The Life and Times of Dinah Marton

My First Kill

By

Bruce, R.F.

The Life and Times of Dinah Marton - *My First Kill*

Grateful acknowledgment is made to the following for permission to reprint copyrighted materials:

All scripture quotations, unless otherwise indicated, are taken from the Holy Bible, New International Version®, NIV®. Copyright ©1973, 1978, 1984, 2011 by Biblica, Inc.™ Used by permission of Zondervan. All rights reserved worldwide. www.zondervan.com The "NIV" and "New International Version" are trademarks registered in the United States Patent and Trademark Office by Biblica, Inc.™

Amazing Grace John Newton, *pub.* 1779 *v. 7 by* Anonymous/Unknown, *pub.* 1829.

Cover Design by Patrick Barrett. 2024.

ISBNs:
Paperback: 978-1-7331318-4-1
Hardcover: 978-1-7331318-5-8
eBook: 978-1-7331318-6-5
Audiobook: 978-1-7331318-7-2

Printed by Lightning Source, Ingram Spark, and Amazon, in the United States of America.

Published by Bruce Books.
Revised May 3rd, 2024, by Bruce, R.F.
www.BruceBooks.com.

Chapter 1

"Fast Forward"

It's dark. It's said the beginning is always dark, but that's not what I'm facing now. The hall, though poorly lit, as I walk down the length of it, looks as if it could go on for miles, and a part of me hopes that it will. So I take my time, as much as I can, with slow arduous steps, which echo, resonating the loud clap of the hard soles of my brown, tattered, leather boots—standard issue where I am, but no shank. I know because I checked, but of course, they couldn't honestly allow that sort of thing here.

Like the ticking of a clock, the sound of my steps bounces off the walls as I move forward, slowly counting down the seconds. There's a light at the end of this tunnel, skewed and slightly out of focus. A glimmer of false hope, perhaps—yet a prelude of what I have yet to experience… of what is waiting for me.

I dare not look at my escorts, who march on, just inches—maybe a foot or so behind me. Such a gesture might be grounds to set them off prematurely, and no woman likes it when men come early. Instead, I keep my eyes front—staring at the tiny, little, metal door that continues to grow bigger and bigger down at the far end. I suppose it's too late for them to change their minds. Perhaps so, or it would have happened by now.

Chapter 1

The metal door, which is now much larger with the change in my perspective, swings open with a grinding shriek as I come up on it. A uniformed woman stands holding the door on the opposite side of the threshold. It is a different environment entirely: bright, cold, and sterile with matte-white paint covering the underlying cinderblocks of the walls—nothing at all like the dark and dusty mile of cored concrete that I had just crossed.

Now inside, they walk me to the center of the small room to seat me in an old-fashioned wooden chair facing a large double-paned window that casts a perfect watermarked reflection of me and the room overlaying the audience, watching from the other side. Most of the faces I don't recognize, and there are some I don't want to see.

Affixing me in the chair, they buckle my hands and waist, and then pull off my boots before fastening my ankles. The guards each take a peek and give me an odd look for the contraband that is my scrunched, knee length, blue socks, and I, in turn, offer a wink at the guard kneeling before me. Hopefully he's getting a good whiff down there. It's not like I was able to get more than the one pair and I refuse to wear the god-awful, uncomfortable things that they issue here. Those too are quickly removed, and my feet placed on a freezing cold metal plate, meant to ground me. So much for self-expression.

Once the guards are satisfied that I am not going anywhere, they let me sit for a moment or two before a man with a razor appears behind me. I think they do this on purpose: let you get a last look at yourself staring back at you from your own reflection... maybe... maybe not. But I will take this opportunity to stare into my own brown eyes and admire my petite self and neck length brown hair, slightly parted over my brow. I'm vain, I know, but after three years of not being allowed to see my face, who could blame me?

So, I turn my head, catching a glimpse of the scar running vertically up the side of my left temple, and then lift my chin for a look at the pale remnants of a Y-shaped gash across my throat. To think, I had already tried twice: once when they caught me, and again shortly after. But now that I'm here...

I'm not thinking of my crimes. As far as I am concerned, I did what I felt was right or at least... right for me. The world is probably better for it. Instead, my mind wanders as I sit here wondering... debating really, if this will hurt, how much, if at all, and if there will be anything afterward? I can't imagine not being here, although I would be lying if I ever claimed to be religious. But most of all, I am thinking back to my moments with him and how he made me feel.

As the man with the razor begins to cut, I say goodbye to my beautiful brown hair. My teeth grit as I grimace and wince at the snagging, tugging, and pulling—and the only tears to reach my eyes are those caused by the asshole with the dull razor pulling my hair out. In this moment, I wish that they'd hurry up and flip the switch early, lest I break out and cut this fucker with his own blade.

Now that my hair is gone, and I resemble Ripley, the electrodes come next. They hook them to various places on my body but mostly in areas that will likely result in death. The female officer unzips my jumper down to my sternum to stick a few just above my breasts, near where my heart should be. And her touch, as innocent or intentional as it is, reminds me of those intimate moments and passionate nights that made me feel so very much alive, but no more alive than I was with him.

"As I walk through the valley of the shadow of death, I shall fear no evil..." the priest chants softly over the intercom. I would tell him to just skip it, that his faith is lost on me. Yet, this moment of prayer offers me just a few more minutes, if just a few. So, I let him. His droll words are oddly soothing to me in their monotone cadence that fades into a delicate veil of white noise, allowing me to drift.

Then steadily, I begin to hum a tune as my voice grows audible and "Amaa-zzing grace, how sweet the sound that saved a wretch, like me. I once was lost but now I am found. Was blind, but now I see..." a beautiful verse escapes my lips, spewing forth the only song of worship I ever liked. Not long after, the voice of the priest creeps in, following in time with me. And as I call in chorus hymn, I imagine *him* being here. A ghosted form, maybe staring at me from the audience—or better yet... behind me now, whispering into my ear—telling me, *"It will be alright."*

Out of all the nameless, faceless shadows casting hypocritical judgments upon me now, the only face I wish were present is his. Not that I want him to see me this way, but selfishly, I want one last chance to look into his eyes, tell him that I love him, and maybe... just maybe, this once, he would reciprocate. A girl can dream, can't she?

A sharp, rough voice pulls me out of my delirious delusion of a daydream like a drum pounding next to my ear, and I stare up annoyingly at the intercom before casting my gaze on the well-dressed man, who stands center stage of the crowd just beyond the window.

"Dinah Ann Marton!" the warden calls out loudly as if his intentions are to deafen me, and he might if I have to listen to him much longer. "You shall be executed via the electric chair as it has been determined by a jury of your peers in accordance with Florida State Law," he tells me, while stating the obvious.

"Yes, I realize this, you pompous ass," I mutter, heatedly, under my breath. I always wondered why they felt it necessary to repeat this stuff. It's not like I wasn't there at the trial.

"Before this sentence is carried out, you may make a final statement," the warden offers me what is, perhaps, a shot at redemption. As genuine as his offer may be, there really isn't much to say. Everyone here knows what I am guilty of. Even to this day, I am not remorseful. There is nothing to be sorry about, at least with this. So, the only thoughts on my mind at this point are those that I've had the last three years—for he promised me. He promised.

As my thoughts circle and my emotions stew, I swallow down that torment for the sake of not shedding a tear to give this asshole any sense of satisfaction. I decide to open up, for there is something I would like to express, now that the opportunity is there.

"I do have something to say, but I also have a request if that is alright?" I present to him. He nods with a slight tilt of his head and a lowering of his eyes before I begin. "The people that I've been convicted of killing were all criminals. All of them repeat offenders, and some of them killers themselves. Where would the world be today if I hadn't taken out the trash?" I express briefly with a pause. It's a hard thing to admit, even now when it doesn't matter.

"Mrs. Gillis, when your daughter's best friend Emily was raped and murdered by a well-known and convicted pedophile that later came for your daughter, Sarah, six years after his release on an appeal over faulty evidence… I stopped him.

Mr. Williams, the drunk driver that crippled your wife, Debra, along with eight other accident victims due to his obsessive need to drink and drive, is no longer roaming the streets just waiting to run over someone else. And warden, you can't forget about the 49th Street shootout that resulted in eleven officers and nine civilians being critically injured—an act that was perpetrated by three gunmen, two of which were thought to have been killed by Pinellas County Officers, while the third managed to get away. In truth, I am responsible for ending all three of them. But, hey… don't take my word for it, that's what ballistics is for." I exhale heatedly. "If you look at the list of those that I've slain, everyone on there we, as a society, are better off without," I say, boldly at the end of my rant.

He looks at me with such harsh disdain and contempt. "You had a request?" he asks, though I am sure at this point, he didn't want to.

"Yes. Leave the bag off. I want them to look into my eyes and watch my face melt. I want my last remaining moments seared into their souls just as my victims have been to mine, for every time you take a life you lose a part of yourself. Do any of you really believe you are any better than me as you sit here, watching now? Don't fool yourself into thinking that this officially sanctioned event is anything less than a public display of murder concealed by an accepted, convenient, euphemism—execution. And all of you are soon to be guilty by association—accomplices, if you will.

Chapter 1

So, if you've come to watch me burn, then watch—if, in knowing the truth, you can stomach it."

With the end of that, the head strap comes on and I can feel the wetness of the sponge they placed between the skullcap and my scalp—a thing I thought they only used in the movies. The water running down my face, neck, back, and chest is a gross feeling. It smells awful, like it was left over from a used mop bucket. I can feel the coolness of that nasty liquid touching me in places and seeping into crevices I'd rather it didn't. I guess the water is supposed to make this go faster. Lucky me. The metal door to my right slams shut as the guards leave me alone in this dangerous place.

I stare at the executioner, who stands in the far back area of the audience in a small booth with a window that he peers through. He wears a black hood much like the one I was supposed to wear. Perhaps he is superstitious about me haunting him afterwards if I saw his face.

I can't help but feel slightly unnerved in the anticipation of what I am expecting to come. My heart is beyond calming at this point, and my breath is heavy, getting heavier as I stare through my reflection onto them. The only comfort I can draw is in the hint of sapphire that glistens from his eyes, visible through the holes of the shroud. It makes me think of him again. Then, something sinks in my chest as the warden steps away and I hear the officer in charge.

"Dr. Marton, you shall now be electrocuted until it is determined that you are dead. May God have mercy on your soul."

I stare for what seems like forever at the executioner's hand, waiting for that final moment. I keep thinking maybe my high-priced lawyer will bust through the door right in the nick of time with some sort of court order. It's a long shot, but I can't extinguish that little bit of hope just yet.

So, let us go back to the beginning… the real beginning… before this. I'm sure you've gathered by now that this is not how it starts but where it's most likely to end. So, let's back up a little. Shall we?

Chapter 2

"Victims, Aren't We All?"

I will start by introducing myself. Hello…
my name is Dr. Dinah Ann Marton—a doctor of
criminal psychology, or so I was.

I was born September 10th, 1983. That
makes me a Virgo, if you didn't know, which
means I am a natural pain in the ass—inquisitive,
though generally good natured. Of course, not
every prediction is accurate.

I'm the kind of person who likes to observe
people, which would likely explain why I chose the
career that I did. My name, too, bears some ironic
significance. The name "Dinah" is considered a
biblical name. In Hebrew it means "to judge" or
"one who judges." With what you may know of me
already, I'd say it was given accurately. Except, I
do not think my parents really intended it that way.

My name in its entirety could mean "the
favored one of god who brings judgment and war,"
but that's really a play on the various meanings of
my first, middle, and last names.

As for the "O" in Marton, I have no idea. If
I had to guess, I'd say it's false Irish, kind of like
the difference between "Mc" and "Mac." My
ancestors probably migrated from wherever to
Ireland, adopted an Irish name but were forced to
change it somehow to show they weren't of blood.

My childhood started off rather typical, living in San Francisco where I was born. I am an only child, and spoiled a little I guess, though I don't think I was a bratty kid.

My parents: Paul and Claire Marton, were a young couple in their mid-twenties, at least, that's what the records show. I didn't know them very well, and the memory is more than half-faded now. But I'll never forget their faces.

It was the summer of 1986, just weeks before my third birthday. We were on our first road trip to Disneyland, and I was so excited to see a giant talking rat as I sat there in the back seat butchering road songs with my Mickey Mouse stuffy in hand.

"Row, row, row, your boat!" my parents sang with me barely keeping tune, "Genly drwown a stweem!"

Mom was reaching back clapping and giving me attention, while Dad drove and sang with frequent peeks back at me through the rearview mirror. The travel plan was to ride along the San Andreas Fault all the way down into Los Angeles. It's quite the drive, and I'm sure they had their hands full keeping me entertained.

"Merrwy, merrwy, merrwy, merrwy, liffs buutt a dwweeeam!" I sang and laughed. "Again! Again!" I cheered, excitedly, tossing my Mickey Mouse high into the front seat. Mom gasped with a startle and Dad jerked the wheel. It was like an explosion had gone off with loud bangs and hard smashes from all over. Glass flew everywhere as the windows burst. I couldn't tell where was up or down until the car rocked to a halt, and I found myself dangling, suspended upside down from the straps of my car seat.

"Mommy? Mmoommy!" I cried, coughing through the billowing dust and smoke, and I rubbed my eyes trying to see past the clouds of settling dirt that swirled with the glare of light coming in from the twisted, shattered windows.

All I could see was the backs of their seats pressed firmly against a crumpled, glass-covered, ceiling, and there was a dinging sound. Ding! Ding! Ding! What was that? Where were my parents?

"Mommy? Daddy?" I didn't understand: why wouldn't they answer? This seat hurts with the straps digging under my arms and between my legs. I'm stuck and the ground is far. I don't want to fall. Get me down.

"Get me down! Get me down!" I cried, but they wouldn't… they didn't. I looked around. The ground wasn't that far. I could almost touch it. I felt around for the button on my buckle—click—plop!

There was a soft crunch under me as I landed. Beside me was a hard rocky wall and ahead was a bright blinding light. I could feel the glass beneath my hands as I crawled and the hot rough road as I pulled myself out of the mangled window.

As my eyes adjusted, I saw her. "Mommy?" She was just lying there on her side, halfway out her window with the door partially open, and her back toward me.

"Mommy, wake up!" I rocked her shoulder, but she didn't respond. She was warm to the touch, and her blouse was red and sticky.

"Wake up! Wake up!" I screamed, desperately shaking her, and then she rolled toward me—her face smashed, her right eye missing. Mom looked like she had seen better days, and Dad wouldn't wake up either. He was locked in his seat with his shoulders pinned to the ground and his head sideways.

The section of road we crashed on was pretty remote with several segments without guardrails, so there were no obvious signs that an accident had even happened unless you looked down into the gully where we landed. By all accounts, I was there for three days, but it felt a hell of a lot longer than that.

Chapter 3

"Recovery"

By the time they found me, I was dehydrated, starving, and numb to everything. Food had no taste, and I couldn't feel anything... emotionally, anyway. I didn't want to.

I remember the commotion very well: they pulled me off my mom and rushed me in to be worked on. People poked and prodded me from every angle—doctors... police.

Eventually, they shipped me off to some group home ran by a large black woman named Mrs. White. She was nice. We didn't talk much, well... I didn't talk at all for a while. There was just so much going on, so many changes. I spent most of my time there under the direct care of Dr. Julianne Bennett, a child psychologist, and for about six weeks that was my new normal.

"Dinah?" Julianne said, sweetly, while maneuvering to get a glimpse into my eyes from my unblinking downward stare. There weren't any tears. I couldn't have cried if I wanted to—and let's be clear, I didn't want to. Crying... moving... breathing... all those things meant I might feel something. But if I sat still, quiet, I could feel nothing... think about nothing.

The doctors all said I was in shock, but I knew exactly where I was: I was in hell for killing my parents, and I couldn't change it.

One day, a couple in their early thirties came by with a specific request: to see me. I don't know all the details, just what I've managed to piece together from various conversations over the years. Allen and Diane Rickman, no relation, wanted a child, a girl, and three years old was the perfect age.

They had been trying for some time, but whether it was her or him… they couldn't conceive. The two of them were concert musicians: he played the violin, and she played the piano. After an event about a week prior to their visit, a friend of Diane's—a woman named Carol, who worked for the state foster system, came running up backstage.

"Diane!" Carol yelled with pounding steps, catching Diane and Allen on their way out. They turned, and Carol offered Diane a slip of paper. Diane glanced down at it for a second and her face glowed with a look to Allen, then back to Carol.

"Is this real?" she asked with repressed excitement in her voice. Carol nodded with a smile, and Diane leapt to Allen with an enthusiastic embrace. From what I am told, they called to make the arrangements the following morning, but got quite the runaround. It took several days to get through.

Mrs. White wasn't happy when they arrived. Not because she didn't want a home for me, but because…

"When you called, you specifically asked for little Dinah Marton," Mrs. White presented, as she led them into her office. Diane and Allen each took their seats in front of her desk.

"Uh, yes," Diane said.

"Where did you hear about her?" she requested, and Diane and Allen looked to each other for a moment.

"Wh-why does that matter?" Allen asked.

"This is not a puppy mill, Mr. Rickman, we're not in the business of advertising our children," she said.

Diane sighed. "I… I have a friend in the state office. She knows our situation." Diane looked at Allen.

"I see," said Mrs. White. "Why her?"

"Well, we wanted a girl," Allen said.

"And she's the perfect age," Diane added.

"And your home, it's…" Mrs. White began when Allen spoke up.

"Oh, yes, um… it's a good size—four bedrooms, well… three. We turned the downstairs room into a music… room—" he looked at Diane, who was shaking her head and he stopped speaking.

"We bought it to start a family." Diane said to Mrs. White. "Can we see her?" she asked.

Mrs. White sighed. "Why do you feel adoption is right for you?" she asked.

"Well, we…" Allen and Diane looked at each other again.

"We've tried everything else," she said with a sort of sadness in her voice.

Mrs. White pressed a button on the large office phone on her desk. There was a brief pause, an audible click, and then a voice on the other side.

"Yes?"

"Come in please," Mrs. White said, and a few seconds later, a woman entered the office. Mrs. White stood and gestured to her. "Mr. and Mrs. Rickman, I'd like you to meet Dinah's counselor, Dr. Julianne Bennett," she said.

"Wh-wh-why does she need a counselor?" Allen asked with a shaky voice of concern.

Dr. Bennett and Mrs. White gave them the dime tour of the facility as they brought them up to speed on the shocking details of the last month and a half of my life; it was almost too much for them.

Diane covered her mouth as she listened. Allen held her close.

"What does that do to a kid?" he asked.

"Most of the children who come to us are damaged. Some more than others," Mrs. White said as they stopped just outside the recreation hall where a bunch of the kids were off doing various things: stacking blocks, throwing balls, running around, but I was sitting by myself, not really watching the others.

Diane looked in with a shocked expression on her face. "She doesn't... play?"

Dr. Bennett sighed. "No. She might in time. You have to understand, her world view has been drastically altered. When she came to us several weeks ago, she was completely catatonic. She's talking now, but only a few words here and there," she said.

Diane turned to Allen with immense pity. "Oh, Allen," she said.

"Kids like her need a fresh start with a loving family," said Mrs. White.

Allen shook his head and pulled Diane aside. "Honey," he looked back into the room with trepidation, "I don't know… maybe… we should wait," he suggested.

Dr. Bennett stepped close to them. "This isn't the best environment for her. She needs a family."

"I…" Allen hesitated, "I don't know."

"If she stays here, she'll likely be institutionalized," Dr. Bennett said, and Diane's face grew puffy and red.

"Allen, please?" she begged, and that's how it happened, or so I am told. Of course, I didn't find that out until much later. My age and circumstances helped speed up the adoption process, and soon I was walking into a big house with new parents.

"This is home," Allen said as Diane guided me by the hand into a wide-open space with a large staircase in the middle. The kitchen was partitioned into a separate open room to the right, and I could see a baby grand piano in another room with big windows to the left and behind the stairs. This… would do, I thought.

Diane knelt down. "Do you want to see your room?" she asked, and I nodded. She and Allen led me upstairs to a room at the end of the hall. As the door swung open, my eyes filled with lots of pink—pink curtains, pink walls, pink blankets. It was the typical girl's room, I guess. There was a small bed and plenty of toys, but I froze when I saw the Mickey Mouse. It was like a wave hit me; a tear fell over my cheek, and I could feel myself shaking. Slowly, I let go of Diane's hand and backed away.

The nightmares were the worst; there were a lot of sleepless nights that first year with the Rickmans. Most of them I spent downstairs drawing comfort from the cold leather couch as I stared up at the dark starry sky through the large bay windows, not really thinking about anything, at least, trying not to. Sometimes Diane would sit with me. The problem was the terrible things I saw in my dreams didn't go away when I was awake.

The unfortunate, natural recourse was therapy—regular sessions with Dr. Bennett, who had taken an interest in me. I hated therapy. Most of our sessions involved me sitting quietly until the time ran out. I didn't want to give her an inch.

As a psychologist, looking back now, it's easy for me to see what I couldn't as a kid. Back then, I thought it was just torture. Some people love their pain. Not me. I just wanted to forget. There's nothing like having a constant reminder to make you feel all better.

"Hey kid, your parents are roadkill. How does that make you feel?"

"Well, gee, lady, I'd feel a whole lot better if you'd shut the fuck up about it."

That's how I used to think, anyway. The harsh reality is therapy forces us to deal with our pain in a much healthier way than I chose to.

Chapter 4

"Lorie"

The Rickman's went out of their way to keep me occupied in those days. I was too young for school and Diane was reluctant to subject me to daycare, so she and Allen took that time off to spend with me. I really appreciated that.

At first, they tried all the typical things like toys, games, and the park. I remember standing on the sandy edge of the playground, watching the other kids run around. No thanks. I turned and sat on the bench beside Diane and Allen, who seemed a little disappointed. But it just wasn't fun anymore.

Instead, they found other ways to fill my life. I learned how to read and write early on, and of course, there was music. By the time I was five, I had become quite the cellist. My room was now a light blue, my preferred color, with only the essentials: a bed, a reading desk, and downstairs in the music room was a small cello next to the piano. Allen taught me Bach; he had a love for the classical, and I can't blame him.

But my favorite activity by far was gymnastics. I really enjoyed the physicality of using my body. It made me feel in control. I like control. Despite all that, I still felt empty, like something was missing from my life.

Then in the spring of 1988, it happened. We went out for a picnic in the park. Allen had a newspaper, and Diane was reading Dickens. I was having the best time doing handovers on a balance beam in the grass when some boys playing in the sand nearly trampled a girl about my age.

"Hey!" she yelled, spitting sand, and I ran over to help her up.

"You ok?" I asked.

She wiped her face. "Yeah."

"I'm Dinah. What's your name?" I asked.

"Lorie," she replied.

Diane said she nearly choked on her cantaloupe when she saw us together. "Allen! Allen! Look! Look!" she pointed, enthusiastically.

"Hmm… what?" Allen put down his paper.

"She's playing," she said, stunned.

Lorie touched my arm and ran. "You're it!" she said, and I looked at her, confused.

"What?"

"You're sposeta chase me!" she said before running away.

"Ok." I got up and ran after her.

For the first time, I had a friend. We played all afternoon—we played tag, we played on the swings, and some spinning thing that made me really dizzy. When it was time to go home, I was more than filthy.

"Mom?" I ran over to Diane in a huff with Lorie beside me. Diane paused, there was a strange sort of smile on her face.

"You called me mom."

"Can, uh…" I huffed and pointed to Lorie, and Lorie waved, "Can Lorie come over?" I asked.

As it turned out, the Burkes—Lorie and her parents, Gena and David—lived just a few houses down from us. We started doing everything together. Sometimes she would stay at my house, other times I'd go to hers.

"Tag! You're it!" I'd run upstairs.

"No, you!" she'd chase.

"Girls! Girls! Don't run in the house!" our parents would yell at us, and I'm sure we were quite the handful. There were times I could see the exhaustion on their faces and the relief when they'd drop us off at the other's house.

Lorie introduced me to the glory of sleepovers, blanket forts, and Easy-Bake Ovens, while I showed her the finer points of one-handed cartwheels, literature, and the joy of playing Heart and Soul together.

It was wonderful learning about another person and seeing how we were the same yet different. She liked cookies, whereas I preferred fruit, or TV to books, but that didn't stop us from enjoying each other's company.

"And Rapunzel let down her hair..." I'd read as she'd hold a flashlight under the blanket, only for us to hear one of our parents shouting, "Girls, get to bed!" And of course, we'd snicker and stay up anyway.

That's how we learned about the magic of the sunrise—how the night turns back into the day if you wait long enough. It was fun having a friend; for once, things didn't feel so… empty.

Chapter 5

"All Fun and Games"

At the end of that first summer together, we started school, and life sort of fell into a grove for a while. I think it was harder on Mom than me. By then, Dad had already gone back to the orchestra. Mom stayed home another year, driving me back and forth to kindergarten. Then as the years progressed, and me and Lorie were old enough to walk by ourselves, she gradually transitioned back to working full time.

Academically, I did ok. I liked learning so school was fun. I was never the valedictorian, or anything, but my grades were decent. I did my work and usually stayed out of trouble... usually. As a bonus, sometimes me and Lorie had classes together.

What I really enjoyed most about school, though, was studying people and the way they behave and interact with others. It's fascinating what you can get them to do once you understand their motivations.

"Psst," I signaled Lorie, who was sitting beside me in the back of our sixth-grade science class. She looked over and I motioned with my eyes to the two kids: Carl and Sandy, who were chatting by the pencil sharpener near the door. I couldn't make out what they were saying, but Sandy was blushing, and Carl looked anxious. I assumed he was asking her out.

"Do you think she'll say yes?" I whispered, and Lorie gave a doubtful shake of her head.

Right then, Sandy shook her head and walked back to her seat in front of me. Carl looked disappointed.

I leaned close to Lorie and spoke in a loud whisper, "I really like Carl. I hope he asks me out."

Lorie played along. "No way, he's asking me. I heard from Tiffany Spencer that he asked her for my phone number," she said, and I scoffed at her before sitting back with a faux look of disappointment on my face.

Sandy glanced back at us for a second, while anxiously tapping her pencil on her paper. I could tell the gears were turning. After a minute or two, she got up and went over to his desk. Carl's face lit up.

Lorie smirked and leaned my way, while subtly shaking her head. "You're good," she said, as I neatly folded a dollar bill into a paper football.

"Everybody wants something," I said plainly before flicking it into a group of boys, who emphatically dove over each other after it.

Psychology, for the most part, had become a game. I read books on it in my spare time, took notes on my observations, and ran my own... experiments. I had even managed to make my quarterly sessions with Dr. Bennett somewhat bearable.

"So, how's school?" she asked from the comfort of her chair with her clipboard in hand.

"Fine," I said, resting on the couch. "I'm in eighth grade now," I added in anticipation of her follow-up question.

Dr. Bennett perked up. "Oh, almost in high school. You just had a birthday, is that right?" she asked. I nodded.

"And you're—" she continued.

"Fourteen," I said.

She smiled. "Any boys?" she asked.

"No."

"Any girls?"

"No."

She sat back, resting her clipboard on her knee. "You know, you can relax when you're here," she said.

"I am relaxed," I replied.

Dr. Bennett nodded. "Okay," she said, trying to conceal her sigh, and that was a win for me. "So, how's your family?" she asked.

"Fine."

"Do you think about the past much?"

"Only when you ask me," I said.

The goal was to not give her anything to work with—no physical cues, no voice cracks, just plain unemotional responses.

To be honest, this adversarial approach to therapy wasn't healthy. It was just my way of coping with something I felt was intrusive and unwanted. In hindsight, I probably could have used therapy to deal with therapy.

In spite of how much I hated being analyzed, I loved analyzing others. It was the greatest pastime—listening to what they'd say, watching what they'd do. I think the only person I actively avoided studying was Lorie.

There was one boy in particular, however, who definitely got the worst from me. His name was Billy Loomis—yes, like the creepy guy from Scream, though not quite as hot as Skeet. Billy was a bully, and I for one, detest them. He ran a small gang that roamed the halls of our school, pushing other kids around. Needless to say, we'd met, and didn't get along very well. Gloomy, I called him.

"Hey Dyka!" I heard with the "Oaf" and thud of another kid getting shoved as Billy and his lacky, John, approached. I closed my locker and dodged, brushing aside the groping fingers reaching for my head.

"What's with the boy hair?" he teased at my usual short haircut.

"What's with the forehead?" I rebutted, and he touched his brow with a confused face.

"Wha—forehead?" He stood there for a second or two.

John scoffed with a laugh. "Dude, she called you retarded," he said, and I snickered.

Hearing that, Billy straightened up to show his size in an attempt to be intimidating. To be fair, he kind of was when compared to my shorter petite frame, but I was pretty sure he wouldn't hit me.

"Oh, you think that's funny?" He got closer.

"No, it's sad." I turned from him when— wham! He slammed his hand on the locker to block my path. I could feel the jump in my chest, but I couldn't show fear.

"Why don't you go home and fuck your mother some more?" he said with foul breath, and I kept my eyes locked on his; I could see a nervous twitch, and I knew he was just posturing.

"Sorry, Oedipus," I slipped under his arm, "I've got class," I said, then turned away with a concealed sigh for how close that was, just as Lorie walked up.

"Hey, do you have the math notes?" she asked, while rummaging through her backpack.

"Uh, who do you have? Zucker?" I asked, unzipping my backpack, and she nodded.

Billy softened up and brushed his hair with his fingers. "H-hi, Lorie, y-you can borrow my notes," he managed, while attempting to smile.

"No thanks, Gloomy, I think she wants to pass her classes," I said before handing her my notebook. He frowned, then tapped John on the arm before walking off.

"There goes Gloomy looming the halls again," I teased, and Lorie snickered.

"He doesn't give up, does he?" Lorie commented, while pushing her glasses up along the bridge of her nose.

"Nope, he's definitely persistent," I replied, while thinking about his reaction to Lorie as she walked up a moment ago. That piqued my curiosity, and I found myself glancing back when she shoulder-bumped me, teasingly-so, as the bell rang. The action brought me back from wherever I had drifted off to. I bumped back, of course, as we headed to our third period.

"You're awfully quiet today." She noticed, for out of the two of us, I was usually the more talkative one, but my mind was elsewhere, dancing with amusing thoughts.

"What's the game today?" she asked.

"Um… I don't know…" I looked back again before shifting a subtle glance at her as we walked. "You know," I paused, "he's kind of sweet on you," I said.

"Who?' she asked, and I gestured with a tilt of my head behind to where we just were.

"Billy?" Lorie questioned with surprise. She thought for a second, and then blushed.

"Wait," I smiled, "you like the attention."

"Don't do that," she said, coldly.

"What?" I asked.

"Analyze me. I'm not one of your subjects, Dinah," she said with a tone like I should've known better; she was right, of course.

"I know, I was just…" I paused with a sigh as I reorganized my thoughts. "What if…" I whispered into her ear. Lorie smiled.

Behavior modification was the name of the new game. I had been reading a lot about the mind, and I was fascinated by what made people like Billy tick. What was it that made it so easy for them to be dicks to others? Was it nature, nurture, or fear? I wasn't sure, but I wondered if I could change him.

The three of us had chemistry together. It was the last class of the day. I sat in the back to stay out of sight, while Lorie took a spot closer to Billy. At about thirty-five minutes in, he got up to turn in his work.

"Psst!" I signaled to Lorie, and Lorie looked back at me with a shrug. I motioned with my eyes to him as he walked down the row to the teacher's desk. She sighed, and then reluctantly went up behind him with her papers in hand.

"Um, Billy?" she said as he turned around.

"What do you want?" he asked with a tone.

"I-it…" she hesitated, "…w-was sweet of you to offer notes," she said, shyly.

"Yeah?" He smiled.

Lorie nodded. "Ye-yeah," she said, then quickly placed her work into the bin on the teacher's desk before scuttling back to her seat.

"Interesting," I said to myself, making an entry into my notebook.

As a criminal psychologist, many of my cases involved some form of behavioral modification, whether it was to help someone or to lead them into the abyss. Call it what you want, it's manipulation, plain and simple, and that was what we were doing. In the field it was commonplace—a necessary evil. Growing up, it was just fun, and with Billy picking the fights, I had no qualms about the effects of it.

On the second day of the experiment, Billy was much the same, beating on the lesser of his prey, but he managed to stop long enough to give Lorie a passing nod and me a scathing scowl as we walked on by. It was akin to that sort of thing lizards do when they bob their heads up and down and flare their dewlaps.

After that day, I started hanging back to give Lorie more space, while I observed their interactions from a distance. By that Friday, their causal gestures to one another had become more audible with friendly hellos.

"Hi," Lorie would say with a smile.

"Hey," Billy would reply.

All the while, I was taking notes, charting both major and minor details on a hand drawn graph with the X and Y axes corresponding to behavior and attention over time, respectively. So far, the trend was positive; the more attention Lorie gave him, the nicer he became.

Then, at about two weeks in, I was sitting in the cafeteria at my usual table, eating strawberries from a plastic container when I noticed the nerdy kids around me all smiling and happily eating their lunches.

"Hmm." I noted this in my logs as I waited for Lorie, who was braving the lunch line for whatever they were serving that day when Billy cut in behind her. She turned and they started talking as they moved through the line. I couldn't hear what they were saying—the distance and the noise made that impossible, but they were both carrying on what looked to be a pleasant conversation.

At the register, Billy gestured with the motion of an open hand for her to wait as he pulled money from his pocket. Lorie shook her head, but Billy paid the lunch lady anyway. Lorie looked back at me for a second before thanking him. The two of them then parted ways with him waving as he went to his table with John.

"Well, that was awkward," Lorie said as she sat next to me.

"Yeah," I replied, while offering her a strawberry that she graciously scarfed down.

"Mm..." her mouth was full, "but it did give me a chance to ask your questions," she said, taking in another bite of some odd thing that appeared to be meatloaf on her tray. "His dad is an accountant for a big law firm out in L.A., um... S-Stratton Brothers, I think he said."

"Well, that's super interesting," I said.

She perked up. "Yeah, and his mom is a regional manager at Bloomingdales!" she said excitedly. "Do I hear discounts in our future?"

She was talking fast, but I managed to get everything down. "Siblings?" I asked.

"Oh, um..." she thought for a second then shook her head, "Hm-mm."

"So, he's an only child. Hmm." I sat back, thinking. "And money isn't an issue," I said aloud as I thought about it some more. "How often are they home?" I asked.

"His parents?" she asked, and I nodded. "Rarely. He said he has the place pretty much to himself—he even invited me over," she answered with a breathy chuckle.

I felt a tinge of surprise. "And what did you say?" I asked.

"No, obviously," she answered.

"This is good." I smiled. "This is really good," I said.

"What?" Lorie looked at me, curiously.

"I… think he's been acting out because he's starved for attention, which correlates with our observations," I said.

Lorie smiled and stole another strawberry. "So, what's the game?"

I sighed. "I need more data." I paused, thinking. "Tomorrow, sit with him—"

"Are you crazy?" she scoffed.

"Just for a while," I assured her, "and then, we'll start weening off."

Chapter 6

"Losing an Eye"

Lorie did as asked, she sat with Billy during lunch. She was reluctant in the beginning, but then settled right in. They seemed to be having a good time. The first day went pretty smooth, as did the second. By the third day of that week, she and Billy started walking to class together. Sometimes he was quite the gentleman and would escort her even when it was out of his way.

"Hey, Dy-Dinah," Billy came up to us one day, "may I borrow Lorie?" he asked, while offering his hand to her. She smiled, took it, and they walked off together. I was stunned. Was he just polite to me?

On the surface, it seemed like the work we were doing was paying off, but I was worried all this attention would lead to him wanting more. I decided I could no longer operate in a vacuum; I needed advice. But who could I ask, Dr. Bennett? No. Instead, I sought out my middle school psychology teacher, Dr. Raoul Cartier.

He was a nice enough man with many years of clinical experience. The class itself was small—only about eight kids—most thirteen/fourteen-year-olds would rather eat paint than take a boring psych elective. Still, it meant I could ask away and make my questions sound purely educational.

The topic of the day was Herd Mentality, but I was more focused on Billy's meandering trend line in my notebook. It was largely positive, but any stockbroker can tell you, no trend lasts forever.

Dr. Cartier was pointing at a diagram on the blackboard as he spoke, and even though I wasn't really listening, his French accent always added a certain flair to his presentations.

"You see, in a group setting, we tend to follow the leader," he said.

Brandon, the boy next to me, raised his hand. "But how do they determine who the leader is?" he asked.

"That's a great question," Dr. Cartier begin, "believe it or not, most people don't want to be the leader; it's too much work. So, it's our nature—particularly in a panic situation—to defer to someone else. Often times, anyone else," he said.

"The blind leading the blind," another student said.

"Yes, precisely," Dr. Cartier said, and my hand went up.

"Ms. Rickman, do you have a question?"

"Um, yes, actually—it… it's a little off topic," I said.

"Well, that's alright," he said.

"Let's say you have a subject with aggressive tendencies—" I began.

"You mean, like someone with anger management issues?" he interrupted.

I nodded, "Well, yeah, that works—and you've tried various things with mixed results—some positive, some not. What's the best way to make him…" I paused, "less of a dick?"

Soft chuckles erupted throughout the room.

"Alright, alright, enough," Dr. Cartier said to the class before addressing me. "Is this a, uh, personal question?"

I shook my head. "Um, no, I've just been reading ahead." I flashed my textbook, which was on chapter 35: Behavioral Studies. As a class we were still on chapter 6.

"You've been reading about behavioral modification?" he asked, curiously.

"Yeah, but the textbook doesn't really go in depth; it just covers addictions, changing habits—that sort of thing," I said.

Dr. Cartier smiled. "This is eighth grade, that's a topic for much, much later, but, uh… the short answer is, you can't change a person unless they want to change," he said.

"What if they don't know?" I asked.

"Pardon?" He looked confused.

"What if you just sort of nudge him gradually over time?" I clarified.

Dr. Cartier sighed. "Then what you're talking about is manipulation. Aside from the moral and ethical ramifications, there's a good chance it will backfire," he said.

"Oh…" I looked down at my notes and the subtle deviations in the trend line.

"In which case," he continued, "the subject may lash out or retaliate. Most certainly, any progress you've made with him would be undone, and he may end up a worser person for it."

The bell rang and I started packing my bag. Dr. Cartier walked over. "Ms. Rickman are you certain everything is alright?" he asked.

I nodded. "Of course," I smiled, "Have a nice day," I said before heading to lunch.

Over the next couple of weeks, I thought a lot about what Dr. Cartier had said, and I thought a lot about my data. But everything I was looking at showed it was working. Billy had changed. It was time to start weening off the attention and let him settle into his new persona.

I was sitting at lunch one afternoon when Lorie came into the cafeteria—a concerned look on her face. She made a beeline for our table.

"Guess who just asked me out," she said.

I looked at her, surprised. "Are you serious?" I asked.

She nodded. "To the movies, tonight."

"Wow… w-what did you say?" I asked.

"I didn't say anything, I… just… walked away," she said.

"Okay, so—"

"So, what do we do?" she asked.

"W-we… back off, as planned," I answered.

"Dinah!" Lorie scowled.

I made a face. "What? I mean, do… do you want to go out with him?" I asked.

"Well, no, but—"

"Then rip it off like a Band-Aid before things go too far—"

"But it has gone too far!" she scolded. "It doesn't bother you we're screwing with his feelings?"

I couldn't help but shrug. "No, he's an asshole," I said.

"But he's still a person!" she argued. I hadn't considered how things might affect Lorie. I was a horrible person.

"Look, if you string him along, it'll only get worse. The best thing to do is back off," I said.

Lorie shook her head sorrowfully before plopping down in her seat. "We shouldn't have done this," she said.

I nodded, then my eyes caught Billy as he entered the cafeteria. "Here he comes," I said, and Lorie spun around in her seat. He was headed our way. "Let him down gently."

Lorie got up. "Billy?"

"Hey." He smiled. She shied a bit. "What's wrong?" he asked.

"Can we talk?" she asked.

Billy nodded. "Yeah, sure."

The two of them went out into the main hall. I followed, peering out around the corner. They were standing by the lockers. Lorie looked nervous.

"What is it?" he asked.

"Billy, I…" she hesitated.

He took her hand. "What?"

"I can't... go out with you tonight," she said. Billy frowned a little.

"Oh, that's ok. We can do another night," he rebounded with a pleasant smile.

"No, I mean, I can't go out with you... I... I don't want to go out with you. I'm sorry," she said. Billy held her hand tight.

"Hey, don't say that," he said. Lorie tried pulling away.

"Billy... Billy, please, you're hurting me," she said as he maneuvered her back against the lockers.

"But I thought you liked me," he said. He brought his free hand up to nudge her chin for a kiss.

"Please, Billy, let me go," she pleaded.

"I thought you wanted it as much as I do." He kissed her.

"Mm—no! Stop!" she shouted; his hand moved to the top of her blouse. "Billy! Billy, no!"

I felt something primal creep in. My heart pounded, and all of a sudden, I jumped out from around the corner and slapped him across the face as hard as I could. The surprise startled him, and he stumbled back over his backpack on the ground.

"No means no!" I shouted, positioning myself between him and Lorie.

Billy stared up at me, fury in his eyes. "What the hell are you doing out here?" he shouted.

"I followed you, you piece of shit!" I kicked his shin and he tried to grab my leg.

"Bitch! You shouldn't fuck with me!" he shouted as me and Lorie backed our way into the cafeteria. Once inside, I helped her over to our table. Her hair was messed up and her blouse was torn.

"You ok?" I asked.

Lorie was shaking, but she nodded.

"Now, do you see why it didn't bother me? I told you he was still an asshole," I said.

Lorie just stared off. "Please don't make me talk to him anymore," she said.

"I won't. It's over," I said, sincerely. I thought that was the end of it. But I was wrong.

...

A little over a week had gone by, but we hardly heard from Billy or any members of his gang. The halls were calm; the smaller, nerdier kids, at least the ones on our lunch schedule, were still doing alright. Even chemistry class, which we all shared, was quiet. Me and Lorie stayed in the back, while Billy, John, Brad, and Clint kept mostly to themselves despite the occasional sneer. Based on what Dr. Cartier had said, I had expected something by now. Maybe he was wrong?

The last bell of the day had rung, and me and Lorie started out on our long walk across the football field to the back road that led toward home when she stopped suddenly.

Chapter 6

<hr>

"Shit," she scoffed, and I turned, seeing her digging through her backpack.

"What's wrong?" I asked.

Lorie sighed. "I forgot my chemistry book," she said, glancing back to the rear entrance.

I shrugged. "Just borrow mine," I offered as she started back.

"No, it's fine. I'll just be a minute," she said, then took to a light jog. She tripped. "I'm ok!" she shouted, and I couldn't help but snicker as I walked back to the rear entrance where I waited. I could see through the glass doors that the lights were already off inside. That's when I noticed a growing problem: the number of enemies.

John came out from the rear doors, while Brad and Clint closed in from behind me. This... was new. I let my bag slide off my shoulder with a thud to the ground, preparing myself for a fight. But where was Billy? I wondered, shifting my eyes between them.

"Billy has a message for you," John said, tossing a textbook at my feet. I looked down at the cover: Eighth Grade Chemistry—Lorie!

Suddenly, I heard a gut-wrenching scream coming from inside the building and down the hall—and without thinking, I bolted for the door. John grabbed my wrist.

"Ooohhh, no, you're not going anywhere," he said with Clint and Brad grabbing on.

"Let me go John, this is not funny!" I shouted, while tugging and pulling against my captors like a fly caught in a spider's web, but it was no use. Physically, I was outmatched.

"Let mee goooo! Aaahhh!" I screamed, kicked, and thrashed.

"What's the matter, Dyka?" John said.

Clint grabbed my leg. "Huh, you don't wanna play?

"Yeah, smarty, let's see you think your way out of this one!" Brad laughed as they wrestled me to the ground.

"Please, let me go," I pleaded.

"Aww, do you hear that, boys? She wants us to let her go," John chuckled.

"Hey, John, look, I think she's gonna cry," Brad said, and they all laughed.

"Is that it, Dyka? Are you gonna cry? Yeah, haha, go on, cry for me, and then maybe I'll think about letting you go!" John cheered.

"Ugh! Arrghhh!" I screamed, barely able to move. I wasn't worried about myself; I had already lived through worse than anything I thought they could ever do to me, but Lorie... what was happening to her? I could feel the pressure building behind my eyes, and as much as I didn't want to...

I could hear my own voice crack as the tears started to flow. "Please... please, John, let me go," I begged.

He wiped my tears. "Aww, that's better," John said, then gave a smug smile. "No, I don't think I will. Don't worry, when Billy's done with Lorie, he'll come back for you."

I felt a terrible cold shift in my chest, and the next words out of my mouth made even me tremble, because I knew I meant them.

"John, if you believe in God, you better pray that nothing happens to Lorie because I will kill you," I said, and his stupid grin left him.

"What?" He was taken aback. "You? Kill me?" he muttered with a fake laugh.

"I've done it before." I stared into his eyes. "It won't be today. It won't even be next year. I will wait until you forget, and then I will kill you," I said. "Billy first…" I looked to them, "…and then you."

"Heh, yeah, right," he said, and immediately I tugged the arm he was holding, pulling his him closer, and then bit down onto his hand. "Aaagghhh!" John screamed like a bitch. "Let her go! Let her go!" he wailed.

They all backed away, and without further hesitation, I took off through the double doors and sprinted down the long dark hallway.

"Lorie! Lorie!" I screamed for her as I ran, feeling my whole body shake with each pounding step. I ran so hard and fast that my flats flew off, leaving me in scrunched socks the rest of the way to Lorie's… open locker. I stopped with a skid and looked around. Her bag was on the floor.

"Lorie! Looorriiiieee!" I shouted, and then I heard it—sobs coming from the girl's bathroom. Nothing could have prepared me for what I saw next: Lorie was curled up in the corner by the sink crying with Billy standing over her, zipping himself up. He turned and looked at me with a wide grin as he spoke.

"I told ya not to fuc—"

"Aaahhhh!" I lost it, swinging wildly across his face. He took it like a champ, caught my arm, and then—wham—he knocked me flat. It felt like a truck had hit me; I had never really been hit before. I shook the stars from my head, spit blood, and pushed myself up to all fours on the tiled floor. I could hear him getting closer. I looked back at him, and then drove my heel into his nuts.

Billy doubled over, grabbing himself, and I dove into him—tackling him through a stall door— kathunk—his head hit the toilet, and without hesitation, I climbed on top of him and laid into his face, fist after fist. I punched him over and over and over—I didn't care if he was still conscious or not. That was the first time I ever, truly, wanted another human being dead. I might have succeeded.

A pair of uniformed arms wrapped around me and pulled me off him.

"No! No! No!" I screamed, reaching for him with bloody knuckles as the school resource officer dragged me away.

There was one small consolation, I suppose... I had managed to break Billy's nose, gave him a concussion, and knocked out four of his permanent teeth, which made his face even harder to love.

Chapter 7
"Rebound"

Lorie never talked about what happened. Who could blame her? But that meant it was my word against Billy's.

I got a month's suspension. My parents weren't too thrilled about that. In the end, the fight was ruled as self-defense, and the schoolboard removed it from my permanent record.

Billy, on the other hand, got a restraining order and was forced to change schools. However, without Lorie's testimony, his dad's high-priced lawyer was able to pull some strings and keep him off the sex offender's database and out of juvenile detention. Instead, they sent him off to Roybal Correctional School—a softer place for troubled teens. It was an F-grade boarding school filled with the worst kinds of people; he'd fit right in. Honestly, he should have gotten the chair.

As for John, Brad, and Clint—slaps on the wrist, each of them. Of course, John would never forget the chunk I took out of the top of his hand.

Lorie's scars, however, were far from healed. In part, I think she blamed me. I know I did; it was my game after all. No amount of "I'm sorry" could undo the damage. She became shyer, more reserved, skittish, and our friendship… for a while she wouldn't even look at me. But she didn't want to be alone.

For months I sat by her bed as she cried. Sometimes she'd look out the window in a startle or wake up to nightmares that she wouldn't share, but she didn't have to; I knew what they were.

When we'd walk to and from school, she'd keep her distance—looking back now and then to make sure I was still there. It was much the same in the halls. Between classes, if we didn't share them, she'd wait with a teacher until I got there to provide an escort. That… was her new normal.

There was a part of me that really wanted her to talk about her pain, and I know the irony in that; it brought my own reservations about therapy to light. But I wouldn't force her. To apply what Dr. Cartier had said, people have to want it. All I could do was comfort her and provide a safe space. And I realized then, that's exactly what Dr. Bennett had been doing for me.

"He's out there somewhere, isn't he? Waiting for me?" Lorie asked in a soft dry voice, while staring out her bedroom window. It was dark. The road was lit by the faint glow of the streetlamps.

"No," I said. "There's a restraining order. He can't come anywhere near you," I assured her.

"That's just a piece of paper!" she raised her voice, then looked down with a sigh. "A safety net." She looked out her window again. "Animals get through nets all the time." Lorie started to cry, and I held her.

When I wasn't with Lorie, I was studying. After all, I had a promise to keep. I started reading books on human anatomy and later added it to my elective courses. I wanted to know how the body worked so that I'd be better at taking it apart.

It was also important that I learned how to punch. I just couldn't put myself in a situation like that again. Jordan Parry's How to Strike Like a Marine was a great resource, and I made sure to practice daily. Of course, I wasn't planning on using my bare hands, I just wanted to be able to intelligibly defend myself if shit went sideways.

What I really needed was a weapon. Something clean. Something that would leave little to no evidence behind. Guns weren't really an option, so instead, I looked into knives and how to use them. There were a number of military tactical books on knife techniques at the library. I read what could, but there's only so much you can learn from a book.

I was in the kitchen one afternoon when I spotted a large watermelon on the center island that divided the space between the sink, stove, and fridge. Mom was upstairs; Dad was in the music room playing his violin. My right hand glided over the surface of the watermelon. There was an odd, excited flutter in my chest as I reached across to the knife block with my left hand and drew a butcher's knife.

For a second, I listened, making sure my parents hadn't moved, and then—shclick—I pressed the knife into the thick skin. I imagined it was Billy as I went deeper into its flesh. The juice ran out around the blade and dripped onto the counter. I pulled the knife back out, and then went for a stab—kachick—oh that was satisfying. I had to do it again. I repositioned my right hand to the back of the watermelon to stabilize it as I stabbed it again, and again, and again—kachick—tink!

"Ah, fuck!" I screamed at the sudden sharp pain in my right hand and immediately dropped the knife. The watermelon rolled off the counter and exploded across the floor, sending bits of green and red all over the place.

"Dinah?" Dad rushed into the kitchen. He stopped at the mess, and then saw me standing there holding my bloody palm. I had gotten carried away and stabbed myself. I lied of course, and said the knife slipped. For that I got twelve stitches.

I decided to continue my extracurricular activities in a wooded area just on the edge of my neighborhood. It was a quiet spot free from prying eyes with a couple tattered mattresses, several broken beer bottles, and a few dirty magazines strewn about the place. I figured if it was good enough for... whatever they had been doing, it was good enough for me, and I made sure to make the most of my time each day, practicing how to stab, slice, and cut the various targets I brought there.

Now all that was well and good, but I knew if I were going to apply any of these techniques, I'd have to get up close and personal. I thought long and hard about how I might do it—maybe in a back alley, catch them on a walk home, or maybe sneak into each of their rooms at night when they're most vulnerable. Whatever the method, alone would be best, which meant, I needed to intimately know the routines of the four people on my list: Billy, John, Brad, and Clint, and that wasn't easy. I was a teenager with limited transportation. But what I did have was time.

By the start of 9th grade, I had added stalking to my list of hobbies. I was getting pretty good at it. School provided a wonderful array of subjects to practice on. If I got spotted, I would just say sorry and move on.

My favorite thing was staying outside of people's eyelines—often referred to as the cone of sight—you'd be surprised by how close you can get to someone before they notice, and it's even easier on people who wear glasses: they tend to have natural tunnel vision. In general, if you position yourself just behind someone's ear and stay between their shoulders, you can stand almost face to face, and they won't see you.

Through all that effort, I learned how to track, spot, and time encounters to make any interactions seem like coincidences. I found that when they weren't together, Brad was quite the choir boy; he sang for his church. You wouldn't think it for his size, but he had a decent voice.

Clint spent most of his time in the pool, practicing with the swim team. In the mornings, they'd train together, but in the afternoons, he had it all to himself. The coach seemed to appreciate his enthusiasm and gave him a key. It was the 90s.

John, on the other hand, had an obsession with Tony Hawk. If he wasn't home or at school, he was doing tricks and grinding rails. I could never get into skateboarding; it was just too awkward.

The hardest person to keep track of was Billy; he was at a different school, but his friendship with John simplified things. In the afternoons they'd meet up at the mall before heading to Remor's Skatepark a few blocks over. Arguably, John was the better skater. Billy's focus seemed to be on cars. When he was alone, he was in his garage.

With this knowledge, I had formulated a plan—a personalized death for each of them. For Brad, I would pretend to be a homeless person on his walk home and stab him. The very idea brought a smile to my face. Naturally, I couldn't stab them all. That would be too suspicious.

For Clint, I'd sneak into the pool house, clap him on the head with a brick, and watch him drown. The image in my mind made me cackle.

I'd get John with a happy little skateboarding accident on the walking trail to the skatepark. It was secluded enough with plenty of coverage. All I needed was timing and a well-placed broom handle—or something sturdier.

But Billy, I savored: there were so many options in his garage—hammers, saws, various tools. The one I liked the most was to wait until he was working under a car, which he often did, and then let out the jack. If I was lucky, he'd suffer a little—and maybe, just maybe, I could slit his throat for good measure as he pleads for help.

Despite how much I wanted to do it, at that point in my life it was still just a fantasy—a dream set for some distant future. One day, however, during the summer before 10th grade, we got some upsetting news—a letter from the court: Billy's restraining order was expiring. Me and Lorie were sitting at the top of the stairs at her house. She had her head on my shoulder, trying to hold back her tears as we listened to our parents down in the living room.

"500 feet is not enough!" shouted Lorie's dad, David, and my dad paced around in disgust.

"A kid like that should not be allowed to walk the streets, if you ask me!" he said.

"Agreed! He should be locked up!" yelled her mom, Gena.

My mom looked around. "Well, what are we going to do?" she asked.

David threw out his hands, tapping at the paperwork. "We have to renew!" he replied.

Right then, Lorie ran downstairs. "No! No, I… I won't h-hide behind that stupid paper!" she shouted.

Her mom looked at her. "Honey, he… he's dangerous," she said.

Her dad walked over. "She's right, Lorie, listen to your mother: it's for your protection," he said, rubbing her shoulders.

Lorie stood her ground. "I can't… l-live like this anymore. I'm afraid all the time—and that's not living," she pointed to the restraining order renewal papers, "It's a false sense of security and a constant reminder. I… I just want to move on," she said, and while I disagreed with her decision, I understand it.

Chapter 8

"Richie"

It wasn't apparent at the time just how bad of a decision it was. That came about three weeks later. I was tracking a guy in the mall as he wandered about some sporting goods store. It was pretty fun; I had been following him for about ten minutes when I heard two familiar voices.

"Man, I tell ya, Roybal sucks—it's nothing but spicks there. I can't wait for this fuckin restraint thing to be over so I can go to a descent school," Billy said in a huff.

I left my quarry and slid over into the next aisle, where I could watch them through the shelves. Billy and John were perusing the skateboard section.

"If you ask me, you shoulda got a restrainer on her; that bitch led you on and then blamed you for it—that should be illegal," John said with a pause, "So, you comin to Carrollwood?" he asked.

And it was like I'd been punched in the chest. My hand quietly claimed a screwdriver from a nearby tool shelf. "Over my dead body," I whispered with my eyes locked on them and my fingers tightening around the grip.

Billy nodded. "Yeah, my dad's just waiting for the paperwork to go through," he replied.

He was right there. All I had to do was act, but I wasn't steady. My breath was hollow, my heart was pounding. I could feel myself shaking with each rapid beat. That's when my eyes caught it, the sign for the hunting section.

Slowly, I set the screwdriver down and slipped over, while drying my hands on my skirt. It was a short hike, but far enough in the back of the store that I felt comfortable I wouldn't get spotted. The gentleman at the counter was a heavyset bearded fellow wearing camo-green outdoorsy clothes and an orange vest. It said "Bob" on his nametag.

"Well, what brings a pretty little thing like you over here?" he asked with a rustic accent.

"Uh," Comments like that, I thought to myself, while searching for words.

"You hunt?" he prompted.

"W-well, I was looking for a... self-defense... item," I managed to say as my eyes skimmed the knife case.

Bob perked up. "Oh, well, we have tasers, stun guns, zap sticks, batons—"

"What about knives?" I asked, and Bob nodded excitedly.

"Oh, yeah, we got plenty of knives," he gestured to the case, "pocketknives, butterflies, switchblades—here," he pulled a large hunting knife from the case and put it into my hand. It had a nice grip, but it was heavy and bulky in my small hands.

"Now, that's a buck knife," he continued, "good for scarin, better for skinning." He grinned.

I shook my head. "Mm… too big," I said.

His face went red. "Oh," he chuckled, "never heard that before," he said, taking the knife.

"I bet," I muttered under my breath.

"What was that?" he asked.

I shook my head again, "Nothing. Um, do you have anything that would fit in a purse?" I asked.

Bob shrugged. "Like I said, we got pocketknives." He reached into the case and pulled one out and unfolded it before handing it to me.

I sighed. It was small enough, but it was too slow. I wanted something I could get out in a moment's notice. I shook my head again. "No," I said, skimming the case. "What about that one?" I pointed to a small arrowhead-shaped knife with a T-shaped handle.

Bob smiled. "Good eye," he said, then handed it to me. The rubber grip was soft, yet firm, and I liked the way the blade rested over my knuckles as I formed a fist.

"That's an infantryman's trench knife—sometimes called a punch knife—full tang, stainless steel—guaranteed to hold an edge—"

"Scchh!" It was sharp, I quickly learned with a wince as I tested the edge with my thumb.

"Careful, honey," Bob said before fixing my grip. "Like that. You ok?" he asked as I sucked the cut on my thumb. I nodded.

Bob continued: "Now, it comes with a leather sheath designed to hide under a belt or inside a boot—"

Or on a garter, I thought. "How much?" I asked, and Bob shrugged.

"$65," he said.

It was pricy, but it was perfect. I glanced back at the skateboard section; Billy and John were just leaving. "Do you need ID?" I asked.

Bob shook his head. "Not if you pay cash."

I paid the man, and then quickly caught up with my prey. They hadn't gotten far; the two of them were grabbing drinks at an Auntie Anne's. I hung back a bit as I listened.

"You wanna hit the park?" John asked.

Billy shook his head. "Nah, it's almost 4:30, Richie will be there," he said, but I didn't know who that was. "Let's go tomorrow," he continued, "I'll meet ya there around 2."

The idea of Billy coming to Carrollwood High School sickened me; it was infuriating. How could they let that pervert in after what he'd done? I had to do something. I had to do whatever I could to keep him away from Lorie. The time for fantasizing was over. I had to act.

That night I hid in my room, thinking about the opportunity that had presented itself to me— Billy would be meeting John at the skatepark tomorrow—I knew where he'd be. I knew what time. I stood in front of my vanity mirror, checking the fit of my sharp little friend gartered to my left thigh as I drew it again and again.

"Lift," I said, lightly gliding my left hand to the edge of my skirt to the soft rubber handle.

"Draw." The blade slid silently out of its leather sheath. It felt so natural in my hand. I then motioned, reaching out front with my right hand to where I imagined his head would be—there was a knock at my door.

"Dinah?" It was mom. I gasped, and then quickly scrambled, hearing the knob turning.

"Uh, just a minute," I said.

The door opened and I dove to my bed and grabbed my anatomy book, pretending to be doing anything other than premeditating. I had just managed to open it as she walked in.

"No, wait!"

"What are you doing?" she asked, then stopped, "Oh—" Her face went red as did mine when I saw the image of an erect penis staring up at us. I averted my eyes and cleared my throat. It was better than a detailed list of arteries, I suppose. I stared back up at her, while hamming the innocent look. Please think the wrong thing, I prayed internally as she mulled over her response.

"Uh, I can come back." She turned.

I reached out to her. "Oh, no, it's... it's okay," I said, and she turned back.

"We never... had the talk..." she muttered.

"Mom, it's fine," I said.

Chapter 8

"Right." She sat next to me; she seemed preoccupied. "To be honest, we weren't sure you were... uh—never mind. It's okay to be curious," she managed.

"Mom." I closed the book and set it aside. "What did you want to talk about?" I asked.

She sighed, nervously fiddling with something in her hand. "The lawyer called," she said, her voice shaking. "Billy's going to Carrollwood this year."

She knew. I looked away, thinking. That meant Lorie knew. I was hoping to keep it quiet; she was under enough stress.

"Your... your dad and I were talking, and we'd feel a lot better if you had this." Mom handed me a can of mace.

"Wow." I stared at the black pocket-sized can. It had a keyring on the bottom and an orange thumb-sized button at the top.

"We gave one to Lorie too. Now, listen..." she looked me in the eyes with concern, "...it's illegal for you to have this at school, but we've discussed it with the Burkes, and we agree you girls should at least have something. It's only for a last resort, you understand?" she said, and I nodded.

I barely got out a "Yes" as she hugged me.

"I love you," she said.

"I love you too," I said.

The next morning, I got up early. It was a Saturday, but I found it difficult to sleep in. My mind was too full, too focused on what I was...

going to do—what I had to do… for Lorie… for me. But could I do it?

Sure… I killed my parents. I didn't mean to… but Billy… all I had to do was picture his face and listen to the hollow echoes of Lorie's cries as he loomed over her. That's all the motivation I needed.

I felt excited and anxious at the same time— sort of half sick with anticipation as the seconds ticked closer to the time. At about 1:30, I started out toward Remor Skatepark. It was a twenty-minute bike ride, and I wanted to get there early.

As I raced from block to block, I worked out the scenario in my head—how I would confront him. The only obstacle I could think of was John. Maybe I would get him out of the way quickly so I could take my time with Billy. I savored the thought.

The butterflies in my stomach turned to knots when I rode over the hill and down the slope into the skatepark, which was located at the bottom and sectioned off by long hedge walls on either side. At the far end was an opening that led into Billy's neighborhood, while behind me was the main road.

I stashed my bike and hid deep inside the hedges where I waited. It shouldn't be long now, I thought with a glance to my watch. It was almost 2. I could hear the slaps and claps of skateboards from a couple of younger kids playing on the half-pipe, but no Billy yet.

"Ramon, vamos a la tienda!" one boy shouted. My Spanish wasn't great—something about a store.

2:05? How punctual did I really expect him to be? Deep breathes... I inhaled, trying to calm myself. I didn't feel shaky; I felt alert. My senses were high. My muscles were tight. I kept clenching and stretching to stay loose, while every sound I heard or shape I saw had me scanning and checking in panicked anticipation.

There was a rolling kathump as the boys rode off the concrete into the grass and continued away on foot—there he is! My eyes locked, my heart raced in my chest. No John? I scanned and watched as Billy's skateboard hit the grass. He hopped off, and then walked right past me with his skateboard in hand.

This was it. This was real. There was no one around, my path was clear. I crept out from the hedges and let my fingers glide around the soft rubber handle as I drew the knife from the gartered sheath on my left thigh. I could hear the woosh of blood in my ears and felt sharp tingles all over as I eased closer—within range. I reached up with my right hand to grab around his face as I aimed my left to the back of his neck.

"Hey cabron!" someone shouted. My heart nearly exploded—me and Billy jumped and spun around to the six Latino boys coming down the hill. I thought about running, but what good would that do me now? I hid my left hand behind my back and slid just behind Billy as they approached.

"I thought I told ya, you don't skate here no more," the boy said.

Billy straightened up. "You don't own the park, Richie," he said.

Richie snapped his fingers with a gesture to Billy. The other boys closed in. It was six against… well… I considered siding with them and letting Billy sort it out when…

"Saturday it's me and my brother. You and your little girly can come back tomorrow," Richie said, and I shuddered at the idea of being associated with Billy.

Billy paused, and then glanced over his shoulder at me. I gave him an innocent smile, while slipping the knife into the back of my waist belt—they're not just for style.

"Hi," I said.

"Hi," he replied with a confused look.

"Hey Billy!" John shouted from behind us, and we both looked as he skated up to the edge of the grass and walked over. "What's going on?" he asked when Richie halted him.

"I was just tellin your friends, here, the park is closed for the day," he said.

John stepped up beside Billy "Says who?"

"Says us, bro!" Richie popped a switchblade. Two boys next to him did as well. Billy and John looked between themselves, while I couldn't help but admire the knives. Richie then looked back at his younger brother, who I guess was about eleven.

"Eddie, da un paseo hombre," he said.

Little Eduardo shook his head. "Pero queiro patinar!" he protested.

Richie scowled at him and gestured up the hill with his knife. "Dije vete a casa!"

It would be nice if he stabbed Billy, I thought, watching the blade. Right then, a terrible idea came to me. Yeah... I lingered on it for a minute. I could... "You fucking spick!" Dirty, I know, but I couldn't waste such a golden opportunity.

"Whoa! Whoa!" Billy jumped in front of me with his hands out toward Richie. He looked back at me. "Dinah, what the hell—you tryin to get us killed?"

Well, not *us*, I thought.

Richie aimed the tip of his knife at me as he charged toward Billy, who was blocking his path.

"Your bitch got a filthy mouth," he said, grabbing Billy's collar; he looked scared with his hands out in submission. "All ya had to do was walk away, bro!" Richie gestured to all of us with his knife. "Now ya gonna die!"

Miguel grabbed John, "Hey!"

And then Enrique grabbed me with a knife to my throat. I'll admit, I didn't really think that through. I had to act fast. I fished along the front inside edge of my waist belt for a small, hand-sized, canister of mace—courtesy of Mom—and released it into their faces—catching Billy and John in the crossfire.

"Argh—fuck—pendeja!" They all cursed and screamed as they fell back, coughing, gagging, and wheezing with eyes burning and snot flowing. The splash back from the spray hit me, and I, too, was on the ground trying to see through my own stinging tears.

Richie, Enrique, and Miguel were still down with the rest of their gang. John was getting up. Billy was helping me to my feet when I saw Richie wiping his eyes and searching the grass in front of him. The glint of his knife caught my eye, and I dove for it.

"Get back!" I slashed at him, and he flailed.

"Tu parra madra!" he shouted wide-eyed.

Billy grabbed my arm. I turned and almost stabbed him. "Whoa! Whoa! Hey! C'mom! It's me." He held his hands out, jumping back. "C'mon, let's go. Let's get outta here," he said, and the three of us took off toward Billy's neighborhood. We ran flat out for two or three blocks before finally stopping to catch our breath. The moment had just barely caught up to me. My adrenaline was pumping. My body was tingling.

"Holy shit!" John gasped. "Did you… see their faces? Haha!" He started to laugh.

"Who the hell was that?" I asked.

"The older kid," Billy stifled, "was Richie. Eddie is his little brother," he said.

John stood up as his breathing leveled off. "His other brothers, Miguel and Enrique, run a gang around here—selling drugs to little kids, I think," he said.

Billy panted and turned to me. "T-thank you—ah, damn!" He winced, rubbing his eyes. "That was fast thinking—though, maybe work on your aim, next time," he said with a laugh.

"Sorry," I laughed, though I didn't really mean it. He then stood up like an epiphany had struck him.

"Geez, what hell were you doing there anyway?" Billy prompted.

"I," I stammered, rubbing the sting from my lungs, "I came to talk to you... about Carrollwood—Billy, please don't go there," I said.

Billy's shoulders sank. "How did you know about that?"

"Our lawyers called," I gave a half truth. "Look, she's already agreed to drop the restraining order—can you please not make this harder on her?" I asked.

"Dinah, you don't understand... the school I'm at is a warzone—that shit with Richie? That's every day for me—"

"Good! You deserve it—she's afraid to step outside because of you!" I yelled at him, and his face sank.

"And not a day goes by that I don't regret it," he said.

"What?" I didn't believe him. Was he playing me?

"I know I screwed up. T-the girl of my dreams finally takes an interest and I," he looked away in shame, "I was so afraid of losing her that I overstepped—"

"You did a lot more than overstep, Billy," I rebutted, coldly.

"Right." He sighed and nodded. "Look, I'm begging you." He put his hands together. "I cannot go back to Roybal—I won't go anywhere near Lorie. I swear! I'll even request to not have classes with her, okay? Deal? I... I just can't go back there," he said. He seemed sincere.

"You go near her—you even look at her funny—I swear I will do myself with a beer bottle and claim it was you—you understand?" I said with a stern tone.

Billy nodded. "Yeah. Yeah, you got it. Anything," he said.

Chapter 9

"Falling"

So, I didn't kill Billy. Lorie, of course, wasn't thrilled about his return. She took it about as well as she could have, I guess. The first time she saw him in the hallway, she froze.

"Ugh!" Lorie halted with a sharp gasp.

"It's okay." I placed a comforting arm around her shoulder as I tried to pull her away, but she resisted with a firm grasp on my arm, while she stared. The moment he saw her, he promptly turned around and walked the other way. I could feel her shaking in my arms as she watched him disappear around the corner.

Lorie then turned and stumbled her way through the girl's bathroom door. "Ugh-arh!" she let out a trembling gasp and grabbed the sink as she tried to hold herself up on wobbly legs, while crying through her panic attack. It killed me to see her like that; it was like starting over. I think that first quarter of the school year was probably the hardest for her, but Billy stayed true to his word— he avoided Lorie like the plague.

Still, I wasn't convinced. The only way I could be sure was to keep an even closer eye on him. So, in the seventh week, I had managed to shuffle around math and biology so that I could share a couple classes with him. There was a sincere look of dread on his face when I walked in and handed my schedule changes to his teachers; it was almost satisfying.

Having the same classes also made it easier to interject myself into his study groups; they often met in the media center. I was walking through the rows of bookshelves and tables looking for his corner when I saw him sitting with a group of our classmates.

"Is this algebra?" I asked openly. The girl closest to me turned and nodded.

"Um, yeah, I think we've got room for one more," she said, and I took the available seat next to Billy. He sort of grunted and got up to leave.

"You don't have to go," I said to him. The whole point was to keep him in my sight, so a softer approach was necessary.

Billy paused with a mixed look of surprise and confusion on his face. He sighed, and then sat back down. My presence made him uncomfortable, and that amused me greatly. Sometimes I'd catch him staring at me with a passing gaze or a glance over his shoulder. I liked knowing I was in his head. I wanted him to think I was watching him even if I wasn't there, but I had to be careful—unassuming and reasonably considerate toward him. That was difficult for me, given our sorted history.

"What did you get for number seven?" he asked me. We were working on linear equations. I panned the table, most of our group had wandered off. The only other person had his head down with an audible snore.

I sighed then flipped up a page in my binder to glance at the answer to his question. "Negative four," I replied. It hurt to be cordial, but that's what I had to do: keep my friend close and my enemy even closer.

The effort wasn't for naught, though. As the days turned to weeks, Lorie seemed less and less skittish in the halls.

"You, ok?" I asked her as Billy walked by on our way to class. Lorie held steady, watching him pass her as if she wasn't there. She then nodded with a heavy, though controlled, breath. She hadn't had a panic attack in weeks. It was working.

"Hey, Lorie," said a smiling redheaded boy. She looked with a quick snap of her eyes to him.

"Oh." She sighed, relieved. "Hi, M-Max," she said with a soft wave and a hint of color in her cheeks. He waved back, and then continued down the hall.

"Who's that?" I asked.

Lorie glanced back at me, hesitantly. "Who, Max?" she asked in a sheepish tone.

I nodded. "Mm-hm."

"Uh, nobody, r-really. He's just a guy in my English class," she said.

"Oh," I replied, hiding my smile. It was nice seeing her come out of her shell a little. Everyone heals at their own pace, and I think for Lorie, having Billy present but uninterested, helped her work through the fear that he'd come for her at any moment. Overall, she seemed happier—more confident. So, I stuck with it.

At the beginning of the third quarter, our biology teacher, Mrs. Moore, made a class-wide announcement. "Listen up," she began, "there will be no final exam—"

"Yeeeaaah!" some boys cheered.

"Alright, knock it off." She tapped a ruler on her desk. "Instead, you will have a research project: 5,000 words—" boos were already roaring from the back "—due the first day of exam week. For this you will need a partner. Whoever you choose will be attached to your hip for the remainder of the semester. 50% of your grade is 50% of their grade, so choose wisely," she said.

Me and Billy just stared at each other for a solid minute, while I mulled it over. It wasn't that he did bad work, but a research project meant long hours together… and time after school. What was I getting myself into?

"Do," I hesitated with a sigh, "do you want to be my research partner?" I asked.

Billy promptly sat up in his chair. "Uh, ye-yeah, are you sure?" he asked, and I nodded as Mrs. Moore stirred a small basket of paper slips.

"Alright, class," she playfully picked at the strips, "come choose your topic," she said.

"Don't screw this up," I told him before walking up to her desk. I drew a random slip; our topic was dolphin migration routes. Joy.

Back then the internet was pretty sparce. Sure, you could do some research, but the information was limited, and the sources were dodgy at best. Most of the time, teachers would forbid it outright, which was the case for Mrs. Moore's biology class. So, me and Billy toughed it out the old-fashioned way with books.

We scoured what we could from the school media center. The rest came from the reference section of the main library in town. We met there twice a week after school to do research, take notes, and critique each other's work.

If we ended up staying late, we'd grab a bite or sometimes we ate early. When we got tired, we'd take breaks and just walk and talk. We spent a lot of time working together, eating together... being together.

He was surprisingly good company. The more I got to know him, the more I saw in him things that I hadn't seen. We were similar creatures with similar tastes in pop culture, music, and humor—he could make me laugh, and his laugh was oddly addicting. He wasn't the asshole that I grew up hating. He was polite, easy to talk to, and courteous.

I simply didn't see what was happening— or maybe I just didn't want to, but I was like a frog slowly boiling, and I was in trouble.

"Hey," Billy said softly as he nudged me. I had fallen asleep with my face in a book. I got up and wiped the drool from the corner of my mouth before I realized I had been lying against him.

"Sorry," I said, embarrassed.

"Your dad's here," he whispered and aimed his eyes to the front of the library where my dad was; he was standing there talking with the desk clerk, who pointed toward the back where we were.

"Oh shit, ok, I gotta go." I stumbled to my feet. "I'll see you later," I said, making a beeline out of the reference section to head him off. I couldn't let him see Billy.

"Hey," I greeted with a smile, while awkwardly getting my backpack over my shoulders.

"Don't 'hey' me—do you know what time it is?" he scolded.

"Well, I—"

"It's 9:30—you were supposed to be home over two hours ago!"

I lowered my eyes. "I'm sorry, I fell asleep—"

He craned his neck toward the back. "Who's back there?" he asked me with a step forward and I placed a hand on his stomach to hold him back.

"Nobody, just my lab partner—we were studying—can we go?" I asked.

Dad's eyes shifted like turrets between me and the back corner before he finally turned away with a frustrated sigh. "Who is that, is it a boy? Are you two—"

"Ew, no," I said.

"Where's your bike?" he prompted me as we walked out.

That was close. Even though it was a school project, explaining our situation would be a little... difficult. I doubted anyone would understand— especially Lorie; she could never know. There was a part of me that felt guilty as if I was betraying her in some way but having his attention on me gave her the space she needed to heal.

In mid-April, I got to see just how well she had progressed. It was lunch time. The cafeteria was full, and I had taken refuge at our usual table when I saw Lorie strolling over with a wide grin and a piece of paper in her hands.

"What do you think?" She handed it to me, then sat in her chair on her knee to lean over the table.

It was a flyer. I picked it up and read it. "The school newspaper?" I asked.

Lorie nodded. "Mm-hm. Max is the editor." She glanced at the redheaded boy a few tables over before reaching out and pointing at a highlighted astrics on the flyer a few lines down. "There's an opening," she said.

"Really? You mean, y-you want to..." I stammered, pointing at the flyer, surprised by her suggestion. "W-what would do?" I asked.

Lorie shrugged, "Um, research, gathering stories, you know—that sort of thing," she said with excitement.

"Oh, well, you do know you'll have to talk to people, right?" I asked, and she nodded.

"It's not much different from what I used to do when you were running your experiments," she said, and I was taken aback by that.

"Y-you're right." I gave her a supportive smile, and she smiled back.

"Really?"

"Yeah, it's great. I think you should go for it," I said with encouragement.

Lorie's smile turned into a grin. "Ok, well, um, I'm gonna go sit with Max. W-we were actually working on a—"

"No, no, of course, go ahead. I… I've gotta do research on my biology project anyway," I said.

"Oh, do you need help?" She paused.

"No, it's fine, go. Go," I insisted, and I watched as she walked over to a welcoming group and sat down with them. I felt a mix of longing for the sudden emptiness and freedom, like a huge weight had been lifted. I smiled, happy for her, and then quietly headed to the study hall to meet with my lab partner.

Chapter 10

"You Would Cry Too"

10th grade ended. Summer came and went, yet Billy and me continued hanging out. I kept telling myself that it was for Lorie's benefit—that I needed to keep running interference to keep her safe. Maybe that was true. I don't know. But in the time we had been spending together, Billy had not once mentioned Lorie, let alone, approached her. The impulse to stab him had faded into some quiet place, and I guiltily found myself looking for excuses to see him.

At the start of 11th grade, my chaotic little world had settled into a sort of normalcy, once again. Lorie was getting along just fine playing reporter for the school newspaper—albeit, a little annoying at times with her pad and pen always in at the ready, and I secretly suspected that she and Max were more than just friends, though she hadn't said anything, and I didn't want to pry.

But the big event of the year was my sixteenth birthday. I think every girl has a sweet sixteen, and I was no different. My parents had gone all secretive, plotting and planning, leading up to the big day, and then on the afternoon of September 10th, 1999, the celebration began.

Our backyard was dressed with blue and silver decorations—my two favorite colors, big banners of happy birthday, an enormous cake, and a crowd filled with people I hardly knew—relatives of my parents—not mine, of course.

"Haaapppyyy biitirthday tooo yoouuu," they all sang in annoying fashion as Mom lit all sixteen candles with her torch lighter and slid the pastry of fire close to my face.

Dad pressed a button on an automatic camera then rushed in with me, Lorie, Mom, the Burkes, and the rest of the family behind us. There was a bright flash, and then a shoulder bump from Lorie, who smiled warmly.

"So, birthday girl," she said, eyeing the cake, "what are you gonna wish for?" she asked.

I smiled, taking in how brightly she was glowing. Lorie was like her old self again. "It came true already," I said before blowing out the candles.

Right then there was a tink-tink-tink sound, and we all looked to my dad, who was tapping a fork to his wineglass.

"Ladies and gentlemen, family, friends," Dad looked amongst us, "I'd like to propose a toast to our lovely daughter on this very special day. Dinah, your mother and I have had the privilege of watching you blossom into the wonderful young lady that you are. Happy birthday," he said with a raise of his glass.

Me and Lorie raised our glasses of sparkling grape juice.

"Cheers!" Dad said.

"Cheers!" we all replied.

There was a sudden clacking ruckus from out front. It sounded like a semi-truck pulling in. Dad looked around for a second and then smiled.

"Oh, perfect timing," he said, and then extended a hand to me, "Come on."

I looked around, uncertain. "What is it?"

"Come on." He insisted and I took his hand as he guided me out through the back gate. Everyone followed. It was a large tow truck. We walked around to the back and my eyes lit when I saw it.

"Oh my god!" I squeed with giddiness. It was a blue 1983 Porsche 911 SC. A car? My mind raced. I couldn't believe it. I gawked at it as the truck driver lowered it onto the street, and then I peered through the tinted windows.

Dad walked up beside me. "Open it up, it's yours." He handed me the keys.

"Are you serious?" I said, and then franticly opened the door to sit inside. The interior was stony gray; the seats were firm, yet comfortable. There was a CD player—an obvious upgrade.

"Now all you need is your permit," he said.

"Yeah, and then you won't have to bike everywhere," Lorie joked.

My eyes veered to the center console, and I let my hand glide over the stick shift. Jokes aside, I didn't know how to use it.

"Something wrong?" Dad asked me.

In the distance, I could hear the phone ringing. Mom stepped away.

"Uh, no, it… it's five-speed," I commented. I'm sure he heard the concern in my voice.

"You'll learn, it's easy," he assured me.

"Dinah, it's for you," Mom said, handing me the portable phone. "It's a boy; he sounds nice."

"A boy?" Lorie made an inquisitive face, and I could feel Dad's scowl from above as I put the phone to my ear.

"Hello?"

"Happy birthday." It was Billy.

"Oh… uh, hi—" My eyes flicked to Lorie, my parents, and my exit as I put the receiver to my chest and quickly slipped out of the car. "It's my lab partner," I said, giving my dad a kiss on the cheek. "Thanks, Daddy." I then walked up the lawn out of earshot.

"What are you doing calling here?" I asked, rubbing the throb from my chest.

"I just wanted to wish you a happy birthday. I thought about crashing—"

"Don't you dare," I scoffed.

"I'm kidding," he laughed, "So, how's it going?" he asked.

I sighed and looked back, watching Dad sign something for the tow truck driver. "Amazing, I got a car," I said, still doubting the reality of it. I could hear him scuffling over the phone.

"That's awesome! What kind?" he asked.

"Uh, it's a Porche, I think," I said.

"Nice! Girly, but nice—"

"Shuut uuupp!" I groaned and turned my blushing grin away from the crowd. I couldn't help but laugh as he teased. "Yeah, but it's a five-speed—and I don't even know how to drive."

"Well, I could teach ya," he said.

"Really, you'd do that?" I asked.

"Yeah, I mean, you got me through biology—hell, it's the least I can do. My dad and I have been fixing up this old Mustang, so you can practice on that," he said.

"You're amazing," I said.

"What are you doing later?" he asked.

I paused at the question. "T-tonight?"

"Yeah."

"Uhh… nothing, I think," I said.

"Meet me at the end of your street at 11:00," he said, and I felt a flutter of mischievous nerves fill my chest. I scanned for my parents and Lorie, who were now starting up the lawn with the tow truck pulling away.

"Ok," I said.

…

I don't know why I felt so excited to see him. Maybe it was the thrill of sneaking out mixed with the fear of getting caught, or maybe… it was something else. I remember dressing for the occasion; I wanted to look nice—a flattering blouse, a cute skirt—not too short, and thigh high socks to put it all together, but I had to wait until the last minute when my parents finally went to their room and turned off the lights.

It was a little after 11:00 when I crept out into the dark upstairs hall. The coast was clear. At the bottom of the stairs, I grabbed a cardigan off the coat hook. It was a little chilly for September, and the light sprinkle made the roads extra dark. I could see the silhouette of a car parked at the end of the street. The lights came on as I got closer, and Billy slowly pulled forward to meet me.

"Hi," he greeted with a smile as I opened the passenger side door to get in.

"Hi," I said.

"You look nice," he said.

"Thanks, you too." He did look nice and smelled good with just a hint of cologne. What was I doing?

Billy drove us out to the mall where we had plenty of space to practice in the empty parking lot. The faded yellow-orange lights tinted the paved road which glistened in the sprinkling rain.

"Ok, what's this?" I asked, while touching a foot to one of three pedals on the driver's side floor. Billy leaned over the console for a better look.

"That's the clutch," he said. "Now, when you turn the key on, you gotta push the clutch all the way in or it won't start."

I nodded, pressing it to the floor with my left foot. "Ok, so key on." I turned the ignition— vvrrrrrrrr—it was louder than expected.

"Ok, good. Keep the clutch in," Billy said then gently guided my right hand to the center console. "Here's the stick." He placed my hand on it, and I snickered. He went red and looked away, clearing his throat.

"Wow, ok." He tried to compose himself before placing his hand on top of mine. I could feel him curing his fingers around the knob.

"Up to the left is first." He guided my hand. "Down left is second." He pulled my hand down left. "Third is up middle. Fourth is down middle, and fifth is up right," he said, guiding me to each place.

"Got it. Ok, first, second, third, fourth, and fifth," I reiterated as I selected each position on my own.

"Right," he said.

"What's this?" I asked, pointing to the "R" under the "5" on the face of the shifter.

"Uh, that's reverse." He took my hand again. "For that you go neutral and then right and down, but don't ever do that while you're going forward or you'll ruin your clutch. Got it?"

"Yeah," I said.

"Ready to give it a go?" he asked, buckling his seatbelt, and I nodded. "Put it into first. Now, gently let out the clutch and give it a little gas at the same time," he instructed. The engine started to rev; the car jerked forward—erk—stall!

He laughed. "It's ok, happens to everyone the first time. Try again. See if you can take it around the lot," he said.

Erk—stall! The car halted again. "Maybe I should drive," Billy teased.

"Hey, I'll get it," I scoffed with a side eye as I tried again. The car sort of chugged, bobbing back and forth as I eased on the gas—stall!

Billy looked around. "Hey, you got ten feet," he chuckled. "Ok, first gear just gets you rolling. After that, put it into second," he said.

I nodded. "Ok." I started it up and tried again. The car took off a bit smoother.

"Good. Push the clutch."

"Clutch is in. Now what, second?" I asked.

"Yeah."

"Ok." I pulled the stick back.

"Let out the clutch. Easy, easy, give it some gas," he said as I followed his instructions. The car kept going.

"Oh my god, I'm doing it!"

"You're driving!" he cheered.

"I'm driving! Woo!" It was exciting. "Oh, shit, what do it do?" There was a curb come up.

"Turn or stop, turn or stop!" Billy said in a panic, and I hit the brake; the car stalled with a screech just inches from the curb. It rocked forward then back, throwing us into our seats. We rested there, staring at each other as we laughed.

"That was close," Billy said.

"For real," I chuckled. "Ooh," I sighed with relief, "thank you, Billy, for teaching me. This was really fun," I said, looking up at him. We were sort of leaning toward each other as we slouched in our seats. He scooted closer.

"You're welcome, Dinah. Happy birthday," he said. Our eyes were locked. "Can I ask you something?" he asked, getting even closer. He smelled so good.

"Sure," I said.

"W-why did you always have it out for me?" he asked.

My shoulders sank as I sighed. "You know why," I said.

"No, I mean, before things got so crazy."

"Well," I got closer, "you were a dick," I said, looking into his eyes.

He laughed. "I was, wasn't I?"

I nodded. "Yeah."

"I'm sorry," he said.

"Me too," I replied.

And then, all hell broke loose. I don't know if it was him or me, but our lips met—immediately, I went for my knife, but—oh... instead, my hand found its way to the back of his head with my fingers running through his hair. I had never kissed anyone before. I had never felt... anything like this... for anyone before.

We fumbled over the center console with the stick poking our ribs as we laughed and explored each other. He had strong shoulders, firm abs, and I was greatly amused by the other… thing that I found. His hand went to my breasts and his mouth to my neck, and my eyes rolled back as I tried desperately to breathe through the wave of ecstasy.

Now I had read all sorts of romance novels, some saucy, others raunchy, so I knew how things were supposed to work, but I had no idea how intense somebody else's touch could be. I was at his mercy, overwhelmed by how eloquently he played the instrument of my body as if he knew what chords to press and what strings to strum, and I reciprocated as we lost ourselves in each other.

I grabbed his face and kissed him more deeply with our tongues massaging each other's. I could feel the artificial texture of his front teeth and taste the metal bridge—and at once, I remembered why they were there.

"Stop! Stop!" I pushed him back and grabbed the hand up my skirt.

Billy went pale, his face panic-stricken. "Oh shit," he gasped as the moment settled. "Oh, shit, oh shit, Dinah? Dinah, I am so sorry!" He stared into my unblinking eyes. I sat there petrified. It was like waking up after a bad one-night stand. I felt immense shame and regret.

"Take me home," I whimpered.

…

Billy drove, while I stared out the window at the dark wet road. My mind was racing through this past year. How did I get here? How did I let this happen? I hated him, and yet…

"Dinah?" Billy peeked over. I didn't want to hear his voice. "Dinah, I didn't mean it," he said.

"You didn't mean it?" I snapped.

He stammered. "Well, I mean… if you meant it then I meant it, but if you didn't mean it, then I didn't—"

"Just shut up and drive," I said.

"Right." He nodded, nervously.

What a stupid thing to say—he didn't mean it. How could he say that? I was so upset. It was bad enough that we were here, but for it to mean nothing—no, I couldn't focus on that. I didn't want to. Then, as we turned the corner to my house, my heart sank even further: the lights were on inside. I was so fucked.

"Shhiiittt," I groaned.

"What?"

"My parents are up," I said. "If they see you, they're gonna freak!"

"You want me to pull off?" He pointed down the next street.

"No, just… drop me here," I said. He pulled over a few houses down, and I got out, using my cardigan to block the rain; it was heavier now. I couldn't tell if I was shaking from the cold or my nerves. So much had happened. I could feel an uncomfortable swell in my chest as he drove away, and then pressure started building behind my eyes.

I swallowed it down, and slowly made my way up the driveway. Dad was watching through the blinds. He looked so angry. Mom was peeking over his shoulder, disappointed. I tried to hold back what I was feeling—Billy, Lorie, and now my parents. I didn't want to go inside, but it was my birthday. How mad could they be?

The moment I got to the stoop, the door swung open; the light hit my face. "Where the hell have you been?" Dad scowled.

"I, uh—"

"And don't say, Lorie's because we called," Mom said.

I looked down. "Ok," I sniffled, wiping my eyes and nose as I walked past them into the foyer toward the stairs.

"Where do you think you're going?" Mom blocked me.

"Who was the boy?" Dad prompted.

"Can we please not do this now?" I begged.

"Answer me," he demanded.

I shook my head, averting my eyes. There was no way I could tell them. "Nn-nobody, just… a friend from school," I said.

"That's no friend, Dinah, that's that Loomis kid," Dad shouted.

Fuck. This was bad. If they knew, then… "You can't tell Lorie," I pleaded.

Mom's face twisted. "Of course, we're telling Lorie—she has a right to know—"

"No! You can't, I've worked so hard—" I almost let it slip. I clammed up and covered my face, feeling the tears starting.

"Jesus, Dinah, are you seeing him?" Mom questioned.

"No! It's not like that!" I yelled back.

"Oh, really? Could you be any more obvious?" Mom said, while fixing my blouse and wiping away the smear of my lipstick. "Did you even consider Lorie?"

Of course, I considered Lorie. The whole reason I was hanging out with him was because of Lorie, but I couldn't tell them that.

"Well, I forbid it!" Dad yelled. "I will not have my daughter running around with a guy like that! What the hell are you doing mixed up with him?" he demanded, and I sat at the foot of the stairs crying into my hands.

"He was my lab partner," I croaked.

"Lab partner?" Dad scoffed in disbelief.

Mom knelt in front of me. "Did he hurt you?" she asked.

I shook my head. "No. He was teaching me how to drive as a… birthday present," I said.

Dad scoffed. "Drive? You don't even have a license!"

I nodded, shamefully. "I know, it was stupid," I said.

Chapter 10

"I'm calling the school," Dad stammered, turning toward the phone, "I'm calling the police," he said.

"No, Daddy, please, no!" I got up, trying to hold him back. "It wasn't his fault."

He picked it up and started dialing, and I cried and ran up the stairs. It was going all wrong.

"Hey!" He slammed the phone, "Come back here!" he shouted.

"Allen, please," Mom said before chasing after me with the dreaded full-name scowl, "Dinah Ann Rickman!" she called, and I stopped dead. I was so distraught.

"It's Marton," I said without thinking, and I regretted it immediately.

"What?" She sounded so hurt. "This isn't like you—what has gotten into you?"

"I'm sorry, I didn't mean that." I turned around to face her. "Mom, he kissed me—but I think I wanted him too." I teared up again. "Oh, God, what kind of person am I?" I wailed, and she held me.

"Did you have sex?" she asked.

I shook my head. "No, but…" I sniffled and wiped my eyes.

"Good." She hugged me.

"He… he really was just teaching me how to drive, and then…"

"Well, that's how it starts sometimes." She sighed, rubbing my shoulders. "Look, you're at that age so… if you want to date, ok, but not him.

Whatever is going on between you two, it ends now. You understand?"

I nodded.

"And you're telling Lorie," she said.

"What? No, I can't do that—it… it would destroy her," I argued.

Mom thought for a moment. "Fine, but you're grounded for a month. That means you come straight home from school, and no privacy; your door stays open," she said.

"But—"

"No buts." Mom said. She hugged me, and then sent me to my room. I left the door open as requested. It was almost cruel, the state Billy had left me in, especially now with my parents checking up on me. So, I lied in bed in my discomfort, staring up at the ceiling. Everything was sensitive: the cool air on my skin, the tight fit of my blouse, the way my socks hugged my feet and my thighs.

Billy's cologne lingered around me, and I could still taste his lips on mine. It wasn't fair. All those years I wanted him dead. I plotted it. I planned it. I hated him so much, and yet the thought that I couldn't see him again, scared the hell out of me. It made no sense. With no other outlet for my frustration, I cried myself to sleep.

Chapter 11

"The Choices We Make"

I woke up the next morning with my eyes encrusted in dried tears. Dad had already made a list of chores for me—cleaning mostly. The house was a good size, which meant I'd be busy all weekend. As a family, we often shared household duties; Dad handled repairs and the bulk of the yard work, while Mom kept to the interior and the garden, and I would fill in as needed. But as punishment, they let me do it all myself.

Mom said all this work would help temper what I was feeling, but by Monday, things hadn't changed. Still, I put on a strong face and began my usual morning walk to school. I had just turned right off the edge of my driveway to the sidewalk when I heard the rapid cadence of running steps behind me.

"Hey!" Came Lorie's voice. I had been in such a fog, I had forgotten to meet at her house, as usual. "Hey, Dinah! Hey, hey jail break—wait up!"

I sighed and discreetly wiped away any sign that I'd been crying, though I'm sure my eyes were red and puffy. Lorie caught up with a notepad and pencil in hand.

"I heard you got busted. Oh, man, your mom called—she sounded pissed," Lorie said with an amused grin. "So, where'd ya go?" She nudged me. "Who'd ya do?" She looked into my eyes and

Chapter 11

her grin faded when she saw my face. "Are you ok?" she asked.

I shook my head. "Forget it, Lorie," I said, and continued walking.

"W-well, what happened?" she insisted.

"Nothing." I shrugged. "I, uh, h-had my first kiss," I said.

Lorie stopped and smiled. "A real kiss? Not like the one Eckles Freckles gave you on your hand in first grade, but like with tongue and everything?"

I just stared at her.

"Wooow," she said slowly, taking it in. "Who was it?" she asked.

"It doesn't matter," I tried not to choke, "I can't see him again anyway," I said, returning to our walk.

"I bet it was your lab partn—"

"Lorie!" I exclaimed. "Please don't pry into this—I didn't ask you about Max," I said, heated. Her face puckered.

"H-how did you know about that?" she stammered. I shook my head and kept walking. The last thing I needed was for her to dig in. Things were bad enough.

I kept my distance the rest of the way with hardly a word between us. At school, we went our separate ways. Since we didn't have many classes together, I was at least free until lunchtime, but even then, I didn't want to be near anyone—let alone, eat. I felt hollow, numb, and achy all at the same time. So, I went off and hid in the study hall, away and out of sight.

I had my head down on the table, quietly crying into my arms, when I heard his voice.

"Hey," Billy said.

My heart fluttered, and I looked up at him as he sat next to me.

"Hey," I replied.

"Did you get in trouble?" he asked.

I nodded. "Big time," I said.

"Me too," he said, gently reaching for my hand, and I reluctantly pulled away. "They, uh, changed my schedule," he added.

"That was my dad's doing. They want me to stay away from you," I said.

"Do you want to?" Billy asked.

"I, uh… I don't know." I should go back to hating him, I thought, go back to when things were simpler.

"Dinah," Billy scooted closer, "am I crazy or was there something between us that night?" he asked, and I nodded. I couldn't deny that.

"Yeah." I sighed, thinking about my feelings. "Yeah, there was," I said. He took my hand again, and there was such a rush of warm relief in my chest as our fingers laced together.

"Fuck it." I grabbed his collar and pulled him in for a kiss. It was intoxicating. Billy was forbidden fruit. Maybe that's what made me want him so much. I don't know. All I know was being with him made me happy—and why not? I spent all that time with him to protect Lorie, to give Lorie space so that she could be happy, and she was. Maybe it was my turn.

I made it to my next class in record time. I felt exhilarated, renewed, like a huge weight had been lifted. Lorie saw me as I walked in, and her eyes followed me to my seat.

"Well, someone's looking radiant," she smiled. "I take it, it's not over?"

I tried not to blush as I composed myself. The emptiness was gone, but I felt too guilty to look her in the eye. "Don't tell my parents," I said, softly.

Lorie nodded. "Ok."

...

It wasn't easy seeing Billy, but that first month was the hardest. I was grounded, and we no longer had classes together. So, we had to get creative. Although the study hall was the obvious place, it was too risky for regular meetings, and making out behind the bleachers, though romantic, isn't as private as some might claim. If we were to keep this up, we had to be careful.

When October came, and my chains had been lifted, we decided to take our musings to anywhere without prying eyes. Sometimes I would tell my parents I was studying at the library, other times, I'd say I was at Lorie's, and we'd spend the night in his car atop the aptly named Cherry Hill.

It was a make out spot for horny teens, and despite its reputation, it was a very beautiful place—wide open and grassy with a sheer drop off to the ocean. To the right of the cliff was a lighthouse, which rested on a narrow shelf that extended about a hundred feet out. During the day, it was a nice picnicking spot with an amazing view and a cool ocean breeze, while at night we could see all the stars, and the warm pulses of the lighthouse made us feel safe.

…

I got my learner's permit that December, and by the end of junior year, I had my license and all the freedom that came with it. Me and Billy took full advantage of that. It gave us the flexibility to work around our schedules or delay our arrivals or departures to make things appear less conspicuous. We were getting pretty good at it.

Then as senior year rolled in, we started thinking about our futures, what colleges we'd go to, what careers we wanted, and what life would be like after high school—and of course, prom. It was coming up fast. Me and Billy discussed at length whether we'd skip it or crash it. We had held onto our secret for over a year. The idea of coming out was unsettling. For the moment, I decided to play the fence, and enjoy the time we had left.

About a month before prom, I got up like usual. Me and Billy had plans after school, so I wore something nice, but fitting for the weather. It was early spring; the mornings were cold, but the afternoons were rather comfortable.

I blew into my hands for warmth as I went outside to my car, and then sighed when I didn't see Lorie. "Figures," I said, checking my watch—6:45; school started at 7. I waited a few more minutes before driving over to her house.

Beeeepp! I laid on the horn, then begrudgingly, got out to knock on her door, which opened at the first knock.

"Seriously? You made me drive two houses down?" I complained.

Lorie smirked. "It was cold. Here, Mom made you hot chocolate." She handed me a mug.

"Ugh! We're gonna be late," I complained as we got into the car.

"Don't forget, dress shopping tomorrow. We gotta look good for prom," Lorie reminded me.

"Yeah," I said, softly, "I'm just looking for patterns, though. Mom wants to make mine."

"Lucky! I wish my mom could sew."

"Eh, it's tradition, I guess. Her mom made hers, so…"

"So, that means you're going, right?" she asked, and I shrugged.

"I don't know," I said.

Lorie made a sour face. "But you already didn't go to homecoming, you caann't miss prom. Max and I are going. We could double date."

My stomach twisted. I needed to change the subject. "How's, uh, how are things with you and Max?" I asked.

"Good." Lorie sighed with a shrug. "Taking it slow." She seemed disappointed.

I looked at her. "Is he pressuring you?"

"No, he's sweet. It's just…" She looked down for a second. "I have a scar," she said.

"What?" I asked.

"Inside… ever since…"

"Oh…" I didn't know what to say. What could I say? "I'm sorry."

"It hurts, you know, whenever…" She looked away, sounding frustrated.

I thought back to when I put a knife through my hand and how long it took for it to feel normal again. "Well… I don't have good advice, but maybe it's something you can work through," I said.

"How?" she asked. We stopped at a light, and I rubbed the scar in my right palm. I could barely feel the difference now.

"Experiment. Learn what it's like to touch each other. Let him learn how to touch you—make it a game, and things will just… happen," I said.

"And you think that'll work?" she asked.

I nodded. "It worked for us."

"So, y-you've?" she pried.

"Yeeahh, we um… we broke the ice on that a while ago," I said, clearing my throat. "But don't rush it. Trust me, there are plenty of ways to fan the flames of passion."

...

Later that afternoon, I went to the movies to meet up with Billy. It was one of our spots. It didn't matter what was playing as long as we could find a dark corner.

I looked around, checking for familiar faces as I approached the entrance when I heard a gentle whistle from behind the ticket booth, and I smiled as Billy teasingly handed me my ticket.

"Young lady, I don't think you're old enough to watch this movie," he said as he took my hand.

"Oh, no?" I took hold of his collar with the other and pulled him down to my level. "What's the rating?" I asked.

Billy smiled, easing close and gently nudging my nose with his. "NC/17." He squeezed the back of my thigh, lifting my leg to get us even closer.

"Mm…" I kissed him. "Then I'd better get permission." We then took each other's hand, got some popcorn from the concession stand, and went into the theater in search of a quiet spot in the far back corner. We always picked movies with bad reviews so the crowd would be small. There was only one or two people down in front.

We sat and made out for a while, not really paying attention to the show. I miss those days.

Young love is innocent… and blind. Nothing mattered, and I had long since given up on what made sense.

There was a soft smack of our lips as Billy sat back. "Hey," he said with a gentle run of his fingers through my short dark hair.

"Hmm?" I wiped my lips and straightened my blouse.

"I want to try something," he said as he slid out of his seat and lifted the end of my skirt.

"What? What are you doing?" I whispered before he dove under. "Billy, what—oh—oohh!" I covered my mouth and looked around for a quick second, and then sat back with my legs up over the arm rests to be more accommodating. My toes curled in my socks and there was a soft thud as my loafers hit the floor.

That was quick. One of favorite games was to see who could make the other… well… by the end of the movie, Billy was up by two.

On the way out we stopped near the ticket booth for one more kiss.

"I'll meet you up at Cherry Hill in about an hour," he said.

"Ok, see you there," I replied, and we parted ways toward our separate cars. I didn't know it at the time, but we weren't the only ones at the movies that day. From what I was told, Lorie and Max were buying tickets as me and Billy walked out. They saw everything.

"Oh, man." Max let out a sigh of disgust. "Somebody ought to tell her about that guy." He then turned to Lorie, who had a painful, petrified look on her face. "Lorie?"

Lorie didn't answer. She just stood there with tears in her eyes as she watched us.

...

Me and Billy laid on a blanket on top of Cherry Hill, watching the sunset. I rolled over and on top of him with a gentle kiss before slinking down to kiss his neck, his chest, and then the edge of his belt.

"I owe you for earlier," I said with a smile.

"Oh, yeah?" Billy pulled me back on top of him and rolled me over, and I squealed with laughter, while comfortably locking my legs around him. He stared into my eyes. I felt so connected.

"I…" I hesitated.

"What?' he asked.

I wanted to tell him that I loved him, but senior year was almost over. It didn't feel right to torture ourselves.

"H-have you given any more thought about college?" I asked him.

Billy slid off to my side and propped himself up on his elbow. He looked away sort of bobbing his head like he didn't want to tell me.

"I'm moving to Richmond over the summer. They have a, um… a really good automotive school there," he said, and that hurt little; it made things too real.

"They have schools here," I said.

"Yeah…" Billy sat up and turned to face the boats sailing out past the cliff. "But everybody knows me here. There's a… stigma," he said with a sigh, then looked back. "What about you?"

I looked down for a second. "Cambridge, Mass. Lorie is going for Journalism, and—"

"Let me guess," Billy smiled at me, "psychology?" he said as he laid next to me again.

I nodded. "Yeah. I can get my master's there and then Harvard—"

Billy kissed me all of a sudden. We held that one—our lips locked for a solid minute before we broke.

"I love you, Dinah Rickman," Billy said. My mouth hung open as I heard him and felt the warmth radiate in my chest.

"It's Marton," I said with a soft smile.

"What?" He seemed confused.

"My last name, it's Marton. I was adopted."

"Then I love you, Dinah Marton," he said.

"And I love you, William Loomis." We went for each other and made love under the sunset.

Chapter 12

"Two Broken Hearts"

The next morning was a Friday. I remember it like yesterday. Me and Lorie had plans to go dress shopping after school, and I was actually looking forward it. I had no real intentions of going to prom, for obvious reasons, but I figured me and Billy could spend the night someplace like a couple of newlyweds.

I did the usual mundane things that mornings require and headed out the door at about 6:30. The sun was barely up; the air was cold. As I locked the door and turned around, I saw Lorie standing by my car.

"Well," I said with surprise as I glanced at my watch, "look who's on time for once." I smiled, but then I saw her face. Her eyes were red and watery like she'd been crying all night. Did Max break up with her? I wondered.

"What's wrong?" I asked.

"What the fuck, Dinah?" she sounded hurt.

"What?" My mind raced.

"I saw you at the movies yesterday!" she screamed at me, and at once, I felt my heart stop.

"Lorie—"

"Are you fucking kidding me? Billy? That's who you've been sneaking around with?" she exploded with pain.

"Lorie please!"

"I've covered for you! I've lied for you—all so you could run off and fuck the guy who raped me?" she screamed and turned toward her house.

"Lorie, wait!" I stepped forward, reaching for her, and she fumbled with panicked hands like I was the most disgusting thing she'd ever seen.

"No! Stay the hell away from me!"

"But you were happy, weren't you?" I pleaded.

"What?" Her face contorted.

"I started hanging out with him to keep him away from you—so that you could heal!" I shouted.

Lorie stared at me, stunned, like she'd never heard anything so preposterous in her life. "You're sick," she said.

"It worked, didn't it? You—you came out of your shell; you report the school news—you... you even have a boyfriend!" I cried.

"And that's supposed to justify—"

"No! I didn't mean to fall in love with him—it, it just happened!" I yelled.

"Oh my god, you are fucking unbelievable!" she shouted.

"Lorie, please," I cried.

"You're supposed to be my friend!" she stormed off. I started after her when—

"Is it true?" Mom shouted, and I swung around to her and Dad standing in the open doorway.

...

What did I do? Where did I go wrong? All I could do was tremble as I sat on the couch, dreading what my parents had in store for me. I had gotten too comfortable—that's what it was—we had grown too casual.

"You better explain yourself," Dad ordered.

I nodded, fearfully. I didn't know what was going to happen if I answered him. "W-we're... together," I said.

Dad's face went a mix of white and red. His eyes rolled up, and he turned away from me. "Oh, God." He started to pace.

"How long?" Mom asked.

I kept my eyes at my feet. "We... we never stopped," I answered.

"After we specifically told you not to!" she scolded me.

Dad sighed heavily as he walked in circles, mumbling aloud. "My daughter... with a... r-rapist," he said with a shudder.

"That's not who he is!" I shouted.

"How could you do this to Lorie?" Mom's question was like a knife in my heart.

"He was a kid when that happened—he made a mistake—one time!" I argued.

Dad turned to me. "Once is enough!"

Mom's face went to shock, and she looked at Dad. "Allen, she doesn't know," she said.

I swallowed hard. "Know what?" I asked.

Dad stepped away into the kitchen.

"Sweety," Mom sighed, "Lorie wasn't the only one," she said.

"No." I shook my head. "Y-you're lying. If… if there were others, w-we could've gotten a conviction," I argued.

Mom sat next to me. "Nobody else came forward," she said as Dad came back and handed me yesterday's newspaper.

"We don't even know if she was the first," he said, and I reluctantly took the paper.

My hands were shaking as I read. "Becky Foster found dead from apparent overdose after authorities failed to apprehend assailant—alleged to be former classmate from Roybal—no, no… it, it doesn't say it was him!" I defended.

"It was him; I called Ben Foster. They just couldn't print his name," he said.

"I don't believe you." I covered my face as I got up and stumbled past them.

"Dinah—" Mom started for me.

"No!" I ran out the door, crying—got in my car, and drove off as fast as I could. I drove to the library and went into the reference section of old newspapers going back the last few years. There was no way they could be right—I would have seen it—I would have heard something.

But then… I felt paralyzed as I stared at a headline dated November 1998—Reanne Muñoz pulled into a bathroom stall at Roybal Correctional School by masked assailant—took her own life a month later. That was a year after Lorie.

"Jesus," I croaked, wiping my tears, and there was another from May 1999—Stephanie Gordon committed suicide when her claims of date rape fell on deaf ears after alleged classmate forced himself on her in a… a movie theatre—

"Aaarrghh!" I screamed with rage and slapped the keyboard off the table. I then sat back crying. Was I one of his victims? My mind flashed back to Lorie, "What's the game," she'd ask, and then Billy, "Don't fuck with me!" he said. Was this his game? Had he played me?

Everything was spinning. I felt sick. I needed answers, and I needed them now. I texted Billy and waited for him atop Cherry Hill, while staring down over the cliff to the crashing waves against the rocks below.

I thought about jumping. Would it have mattered? My best friend hated me. My parents were appalled, and the guy I thought I loved… how did I get here?

I could hear Billy's mustang coming up the hill, and I turned into the wind and dust as he pulled in and got out.

"I got your text. I didn't see you at school today, is everything alright?" he asked as he approached, and I threw the newspaper at his feet. Billy looked down at it, then went pale.

"Is it true?" I asked.

"Dinah—"

"Is it true!" I demanded.

Billy's eyes sank in shame. He sighed, then nodded. Oh, God, I didn't want it to be true.

"Stephanie Gordon?" I asked.

Billy nodded.

"Reanne Muñoz?" My voice cracked, and again, he nodded. "A-am I just another one of your… conquests?"

He looked at me in shock. "What? No, no, Dinah, I… I love you," he said.

"Don't!" I screamed.

"But I do!" Billy ran up to me.

"No, you don't! Don't say that! You're just fucking me—screwing with my head!" I cried as my knees gave out, and I plopped to the ground.

Billy knelt and held me. "Would I tell you the truth if I didn't love you?" he said, staring into my eyes.

"No." I looked away in denial.

"Don't you understand? I love you," he said, and I straightened up.

"I hate you," I said.

"What? No, you don't mean that," he said.

"Yes, I do. I hate you. I hate you for what you did to Lorie!" I shouted, feeling that pain release. "And these girls…" I sobbed.

Billy looked so hurt. "Dinah, y-you said you loved me."

"How could I be so stupid? I don't even know if my feelings are real!" I shouted.

"Don't say that." He gently nudged my face to look at him. "Dinah, I…" he sighed. "Th-those girls, these urges—none of that matters when I'm with you," he said.

"Oh, God." I looked away.

"No, you don't understand. I haven't felt those… urges since we've been together, and I don't want to be that person anymore. Don't give up on me, please?" he said.

"And what happens when we go off to college? What happens when we go our separate ways?" I asked.

Billy shook his head. "I… I don't know. All I know is right now," he said as he held me tight, and I cried as I held him back.

Chapter 13

"My First… Time"

Being with Billy made me a stranger in my house. Dad wouldn't look at me, and Mom would hardly say more than two words. The shame they wore around me was worse than any punishment they could have given. It was much the same at school. Lorie avoided me; she got rides from her mom or Max. People looked at me differently.

"Will you please talk to me," I begged Lorie. Max ran interference, blocking me. She gave me the cold shoulder as he stared me down, and then escorted her to class as if I was the villain now. I wiped my face and sniffled, watching her not even look back. I had really fucked things up. The only upside was me and Billy no longer had to sneak around.

We walked the halls with our hands together and our heads high despite the gawking stares. It was weird. I could hear whispers like, "What's she doing with him?" and "Does she know?" but no one said anything to my face. The wide berth, usually given to Billy, now applied to both of us.

It was bittersweet, though. For a while, our kisses were stale, and I found his touch oddly undesirable, but given the circumstances, he was the only one willing to even talk to me. All things considered, we decided to finish out the year strong and let the future bring whatever it brought. That included going to prom.

But I needed a dress. Since shopping with Lorie was out, I looked at styles and patterns through brochures, catalogs, boutiques, and online. The internet wasn't the powerhouse of information it is today, but options were plentiful. I wanted something that showed off my form without being too revealing—a mid-back with a flowy, knee-length skirt would do—and satin, powder blue.

I ordered the materials I needed, and then followed the sad sound of the piano to the music room where Mom was playing Adagio et Cantabile, to be specific.

"Mom?" I called quietly from the doorway. The piano stopped with a sharp wipe of the keys, and she turned to look over her shoulder at me with a sigh. "I... I know you and Dad don't approve, but... can we still make my dress?" I asked.

Mom's eyes trailed down for a moment, and then she nodded before getting up to prep a space to cut and sew. We worked together, but quietly. She'd use her eyes and body language or would point in favor of speaking to me. I guess she didn't want to start an argument that would ultimately go nowhere.

When it came time to fit the dress, she stood me on a stool and moved my arms up or down like a posable figure as she stitched. I could see myself in the vanity mirror. Despite the tension between us, it was coming along.

"Do…" I hesitated, "do you and Dad hate me?" I asked.

Mom sighed with half-glances at me before answering, "Of course not," she said, while tying a stitch. "We love you, even… when you do stupid things."

That was a relief, at least. Mom moved around me, checking the back of the dress. "How's Lorie?" she asked.

I shrugged. "Avoiding me," I answered.

"You hurt her really bad," Mom said.

"I didn't mean to, I was try—" I stopped myself and played with my fingers.

"I don't understand why you insist on seeing that… that boy," she said, harshly.

"I love him," I replied.

"Ugh," Mom scoffed, "you're seventeen, you don't know what love is," she argued.

"You and Dad got married out of high school—it's not like you had a better sample size," I sassed, and Mom jabbed her index finger with the needle.

"Ouch—damn it." She sucked it for a second, while glaring at me.

"I'm sorry. That was… uncalled for," I said.

Mom sighed. She put the needle down, and then turned me around for a once-over. "Pretty as a picture," she said before kissing my cheek and packing away the sewing kit.

…

On the day of the big event, I spent a lot of time in my room thinking and playing the cello—Mozart's Ave Verum; it was the only thing I could think of to calm my nerves. Every now and then Dad would peek in, but he wouldn't say anything.

At three o'clock, I took a long hot shower, groomed all the necessary areas for the night I was expecting, and fixed my hair. There's only so much you can do when it's short, but I parted the middle and pinned back my bangs.

I had just finished putting on my lingerie and was adjusting the rib alignment of my powder blue thigh highs when I heard a soft knock on my door. I looked over as Mom walked in carrying my dress, forearm-length gloves, and pantyhose, which she offered to me.

"Ugh, really, Dinah?" Mom questioned with a glance up and down my legs as I gartered the top of the thigh socks to my panties.

"What?" I asked, sheepishly, eying the pantyhose in her hand, "I'm not wearing those; they suffocate your crotch—besides," I flexed my toes through the more comfortable cotton," these are cuter."

Mom threw the hose aside and straightened out my dress. "Well, let's get you into this," she said as she helped slide it over my head.

"Watch my hair," I said.

"It's fine. Got the earrings?"

"Yes," I said, with a flick of my lobe before fixing the straps of the dress over my shoulders.

"Headdress?" Mom asked, and I motioned with my eyes to my nightstand. She turned and picked up an ornate string of small pearls, arranged in four bands, and fitted them over my head and attached them to my hair.

"How's that?" she asked, and I looked into the mirror.

"God." I sighed.

"What?"

"I look like the Empress," I said.

"You look fine," Mom replied.

There was another knock at my door, and we looked to see Dad easing it open. "Am I interrupting?" he asked.

"No, we're about done here," Mom said.

"Can I have a minute?" he asked.

Mom looked at me for a second. "Sure," she said, then stepped out.

Dad walked up to me, while fiddling with something in his hand. "I have a, uh..." It was a small pearl and diamond charm. "Your... your mother helped pick it out. May I?" he asked.

"Sure," I said.

He attached it to the front of my headdress, and then straightened my shoulders to look me over. "Listen, just..." he sighed. I could tell he was holding something back. "Don't... come home pregnant," he said.

I nodded. "I won't."

The doorbell rang and I could hear Mom calling up from downstairs. "Dinah!"

"I'll… be right down!" I shouted. Dad's eyes fell in disappointment as if he was hoping I had changed my mind. I got close and raised up on my tip toes to kiss his cheek. "Thanks, Daddy," I said, sweetly, and then guided him to the door.

Once he was out, I finished putting together my ensemble with the final touches being the one-inch heels, and the gloves, and then I knelt down in front of my dresser to remove the bottom drawer. Beneath it was empty space—a great place to hide things; no one ever seems to look there.

I sat on my knees and stared at my collection of private things—among which was an old sharp friend that I had long since retired, and another that I had borrowed from Richie Muñoz almost two years ago. My heart beat uncomfortably as I pulled out the switchblade. I tested its function, and then went downstairs.

Billy looked so handsome in his matching, powder blue, tuxedo.

"Hi," I greeted with a genuine smile.

"Hi," he replied, while presenting a corsage, which he slid over my right wrist. In turn, I pinned his boutonniere to his lapel. "You look beautiful," he added.

"And you're very handsome," I said with a kiss and a hug, and then laid my head warmly against his chest. His heart was beating so fast. I looked up at him. "You ok?"

"I have, um… s-something I—"

"Hmm-mm," Dad cleared his throat from the doorway and gave Billy a very intimidating stare. "You better bring her back as is," he said in a stern tone with a pointed finger.

Billy nodded. "Yes, sir."

…

Me and Billy went to a fancy dinner, and then arrived at the dance fashionably late. It was a nice venue, filled with people we knew—teachers, students—and music from six generations ago—oh, and that god-awful Cha Cha Slide. By then, the spectacle of our courtship turned only a few heads. That was fine by me.

The first thing we did was hit the picture booth to capture the moment under a ceremonial archway, and then we mingled with a few mutual friends—John, Brad, and Clint, who all went stag and were now circling the buffet spread to satiate their boredom.

Then came the slow jam. I remember it being Unchained Melody—the perfect slow-dance song. Me and Billy held each other close, and I rested my head on his chest.

Every now and then I'd see Lorie on the dance floor with Max. She wore her hair up with gold, dangly earrings, contact lenses, and a purple dress. Max wore a black tux, simple but fitting. They paid us little mind, though whenever she saw us, her smile would drop and her eyes would quickly flick away.

When the music changed to something with a beat, I got wild with a booty-dance—a raised leg and a little twerk to get a rise out of my date. Billy seemed unsure at first, but he livened up and joined in. Even John managed to have a good time.

"May I cut in?" he asked. Billy nodded, and I offered my hand to John. He took it and pulled me in with a spin.

"Woo!" I cheered, and we unwound to our fingertips. "Where's your girl?" I asked.

"Just me tonight," he replied before leading me into a sort of tango. It was the wrong music for it, but it was fun.

"That's a shame; she's missing out," I said.

John smiled and twirled me. "You're pretty alright, yourself, Dinah."

"Who taught you this?" I asked.

"My mom," he replied.

"Talented lady." I smiled.

The music changed, and John handed me back to Billy. "Thanks for the dance," John said.

"Any time," I said, then turned to Billy. I was hot and flush from dancing. "I'm gonna grab some punch, you want some?" I asked.

Billy shook his head. "No, go ahead."

I could feel my sock slipping and bunching as I walked and the strap over my arch was pinching my instep. "Gah, damn these shoes," I complained with a hand on the table as I tried to adjust it.

"You're not supposed to wear socks with those," Lorie said, and I snapped my eyes to her.

"Uh," I let out a fake laugh, trying not to look surprised, "fashion over function," I said.

Lorie nodded. "It's cute." She paused for a moment. "You look nice."

"Thanks. So do you, um…"

"Yeah…"

"How have you—" we both said at once.

"I'm sorry," I said.

"No, I'm sorry." She looked down. "I saw you dancing earlier. You two look… r-really ha-happy together." She sighed.

"Thanks. You guys too."

"Listen, I, um… I'm s-sorry about some of the things I said before," she said.

"Me too."

"I was so mad at you." Lorie leaned against the table and looked off as she spoke. "For a while I… even blamed you for what he did to me," she said, her voice shaky.

"That was my fault," I said.

"No, it was his." Lorie looked at me. "He chose to hurt me, and then you were with him, and I felt so… betrayed by that." She wiped her eyes. "But, um… you were right, keeping him away from me… did help—in whatever fucked up way that is." She paused for a second. "I've had a lot of time to think about that, and… I realized w-what you'd sacrificed for me… was your heart," she said.

"Lorie—" I sniffled, and we hugged for a minute, and then we composed ourselves. "Are... are we ok," I asked.

Lorie shook her head. "You're my best friend, and I want you to be happy, but I can't... h-have him in my life. I'm sorry," she said.

I nodded. I understood. "So, what now?"

"Now?" Her eyes wandered. "Max and I are gonna go someplace special, make love for the first time," she said.

"Really?" I smiled. "Y-you're not scared?" I asked, and Lorie shrugged.

"A friend of mine showed me the value of taking risks." She smiled back before walking over to Max. The two of them grabbed their things, and then headed out.

Me and Billy finished the dance strong, and then at 11:30, when they kicked us out, most of us went to Cherry Hill. I had never seen so many cars packed into such a tiny space and along the edge of the cliff. We were positioned just off center of the main path with John parked just a car or two away.

There was music all around us with everybody's make out tracks melding into a single song. For us, it was Billy's Police CD with Every Breath You Take—a great romance song if you ignore it's about a stalker.

As the night went on, things got steamy; we held each other close and pressed our lips and tongues together as we worked each other from over the center console. The windows were fogging with the air conditioning struggling against our rising body heat. I teased at his zipper—slipping a hand in to say hello, and he squeezed my breasts in one hand and returned the favor with the other. I gasped with a sudden moan. His touch set me on fire. I hadn't wanted him this badly in weeks.

"Mmm," Billy murmured and sat back as he came up for air. "Dinah?"

"Mm-mm?" I looked into his eyes.

"I love you," he said.

"I love you, too," I said.

Billy smiled, then his eyes shied away. "I… I know this is supposed to be our last night together, but…" He seemed nervous.

"But what?" I asked with a gentle hand to his cheek.

"I can't image my life without you," he said, while fumbling around in his pants pocket for a second, and then he pulled out a small ring box. My eyes went wide, and I felt my heart flutter. I couldn't believe it. There was a soft pop as he opened it to a small gold and diamond ring.

"Dinah Ann Marton, w-will you marry me?" he asked in a shaky voice.

"Yes! Oh, my god, yes!" I squeed, and he placed the ring on my finger. I sat back, staring at it—did this just happen?

"I love you, Dinah Marton," Billy said.

I moved close to him and looked into his eyes again. "And I love you, William Loomis," I said, and we kissed.

Chapter 13

It was getting late. I could see cars leaving through the fogged windows. I liked the idea of things being more private… more intimate, but I felt like Cinderella. The night was ending; my nerves were kicking in. Ugh… I could feel my bladder.

"Honey," I said, sweetly, "I've gotta find a bush; too much punch."

Billy smiled with a gesture to the door, and I stepped out onto the dark, grassy hill. The lighthouse was shining. Everyone was gone except for one car that was now pulling out and John, who was sipping beers with Clint and Brad. I could hear bottles crashing as they threw them over the cliff.

I wasn't gone for too long, just a couple minutes to take care of some business, and then back to the car. The CD had restarted, and Billy was popping a fresh mint as I got in.

"Now where were we?" I asked, while sliding over the console and into his lap—beep! My back hit the horn and we both jumped and laughed.

Billy took my left hand. "Mm, what's that?" he asked, and I looked at the black smear on the wrist of my glove.

"Oh, no," I groaned.

"Looks like grease," Billy said.

"I must've caught it on the door. I hope this doesn't stain; mom's gonna kill me," I said.

"She'll probably think you were drinking," Billy teased as he turned my chin and distracted me with a kiss. I put my arms around him, and we got back to it. I reached down between us. Billy moaned and laid his head back as I lined him up and—

"Ohh!" My body shuddered with pleasure as I pressed down. His hands went to my back to pull me in as he pushed. My mouth went to his to cover our moans—tap tap! There was a knock at the window.

"Shit!" We looked out. It was John.

Billy caught his breath, and then cracked the window a bit.

"Hey, sorry to interlupt—buurrpp—we're gonna book it. There'sa after parly at Hagle's house. I hear she puts out," he said before stumbling toward his car.

"Ok," Billy said.

"Bye, John," I said as the window went back up. Me and Billy laughed.

"0 for 3?" He smiled and kissed me again.

"Mm." I put my forehead to his. I wanted to be with him in this moment. I wanted to stay with him. I wanted it to last.

"God, you're shaking," Billy said.

"I…" I looked into his eyes; I felt a tear fall.

"Hey, hey, look at me." Billy nudged my chin. "What's wrong?"

"I just… don't want the night to end," I said.

"Honey—"

There was a sudden squeal of tires, a skidding screech of rubber, and a loud crraaassh at the bottom of the hill, and then—beeeeeeeeep! I snapped a panicked gaze over my shoulder; I knew what it was.

"What's that?" Billy looked past me, and with my right hand, I drew Richie's switchblade and plunged it into his sternum. Billy let out a hellish gasp. Blood poured out, warm and wet. His body thrashed and spasmed, and I rested down with all my weight against the knife, while watching the look of horror on his face as the light in his eyes went out. Billy's head slumped back into his seat; his hands fell away.

"I'm sorry," I whispered.

I cried there for a few minutes with my forehead pressed to his. I couldn't undo it. I couldn't take it back. I kissed his lifeless lips.

"I love you, William Loomis," I said with a sniffle, and then gently closed his eyes.

Now, you're probably wondering, "What the fuck?" But when I learned the truth, I knew I couldn't leave Billy alive. It was no longer about avenging Lorie; it was about everyone else he would hurt.

So, I stayed with Billy, and kept him close. In the weeks leading up to prom, I surveyed the hill. At the top, there were some bushes to hide a few necessary things, while at the bottom was a large oak tree just before the turnout to the main road.

The plan was to make it look like Richie and his gang had attacked us, not much of a stretch. I just needed a few tools to set the stage. I borrowed some cutters from Richie's garage, along with an old baseball bat. I knew John would follow us to the hill and likely stick around till the last minute. That's when I cut them. Billy saw the grease on my glove—a mistake.

I kissed Billy once more, and then climbed off before smashing his Mustang to shit with Richie's prized Mickey Mantle Special Edition—a sin against baseball, I'm sure—and then I headed down the hill to finish what I'd started. I knew I didn't have a lot of time. John's horn would soon attract attention.

I could hear it blaring as I approached his crumpled Thunderbird, now wrapped nicely around the tree. Clint had gone through the windshield, while Brad was slumped in the back seat with the window cracked and the side of his head caved in; he never made it through the glass.

John was halfway out his window, gasping through his obviously crushed ribs and broken nose. "Heeelllpp!" He wheezed, and then his eyes widened when he saw me. "Di-Dinnnah, get heeellllpp!" He reached out, weakly.

"Sure." I knelt down to eye level, "I can help you, John. If you cry for me," I said.

John gasped, choking on his blood. "Bi-Billy!" he tried.

"Oh, shhh." I gently wiped his face, "It's ok, I already killed him, and as promised, I'm going to kill you now, John."

He looked so scared. I almost felt sorry for the poor prick. Almost. I stood tall, readied the bat and—crack—crack—crack! I bashed his head until I was satisfied. That one… was for me. I checked their pulses, and then went back up the hill.

To sell the idea that we were attacked, I roughed up Billy with the bat and added a few extra holes for good measure. On his hands and forearms, I cut in some defensive wounds.

With the stage set, there was only one thing left to do: I took some necessary breaths to hype myself up, held out the bat, and—whack!

"Aaugh!" I cried out in pain and fell to my knees, holding the right side of my face. I opened my right eye to make sure I could still see. It was a little blurry but otherwise ok. With a trembling hand, I picked up the bat again, and prepared myself for another strike—kathunk!

"Ahh—fuck!" I fell against the car. I could feel my right eye swelling shut, but I couldn't stop at just a bruise. I grabbed the knife, and with a shaky hand, held the tip of the blade to the space above my right collar bone. I took a deep breath, and then pressed in.

"Gaahh!" It was such a strange sensation; I could feel the flesh separating with a burning cutting sting as it went in; blood poured down my right arm. I needed to go deep enough to look life threatening, but not too deep.

I then held the knife just outside my right ribs, took a few more breaths, and then quickly jabbed in once—"Ugghhar!" and then twice—"Huuarghbh!" I gasped, and then steadied myself before adding my own defensive wounds. To get the angles right, I envisioned Richie stabbing me from the window.

The hardest part, however, was my right arm; I had to break it. I figured if Richie had put the bat through the window, he would have hit my upper arm. So, I staggered my way back into the passenger seat, positioned my right arm across the jam, and…

"One… two… thhrreee!" I slammed the door as hard as I could. "Arghh—hahh!" I cried out loud, but it didn't break. I sat there for a second or two, holding my arm, waiting for the pain to subside before reluctantly trying again—wham—

"Ah!" I screamed. No good. I pushed the door back open, repositioned my arm, and tried again—crack! "Ughaahh!" I felt it pop. My arm slumped, and I went down with the pain pulling me to the floor. It was so bad, I couldn't move. Gently, I lifted my right arm with my left, pinned it tight to my chest, and then shut the door.

Sirens wailed in the distance; I could see flashing lights. The police were on their way. I curled up with Billy as best I could over the console and kissed him one last time as I lied there waiting… crying… scared. I had just killed four people, including the man I both loved… and hated, and I had no clue what my future would bring.